WHERE DO I FIND AUDITIONS?

A Practical Guide to Finding Auditions
in New York City and Beyond

by

David Neal Levin

CONTENTS

Introduction   5

The Internet   7

Meet and Greets   40
Workshops, Classes, and Seminars

Other Ways to Find Auditions   49

Interviews

Casting Directors   61

Representation   88

Final Thoughts   99

Acknowledgements   100

INTRODUCTION

This is the book I wish had existed when I began acting.

I'm sorry, *who* are you...?

Good question! My name is David Neal Levin and I'm a working actor living in New York City. You can learn more about me and see some of my work at www.davidneallevin.com.

What you are about to read is everything I know about finding auditions, laid out as clearly and succinctly as I know how. This book is a more organized and comprehensive version of a nuts-and-bolts workshop I teach in New York called (surprise!) 'Where Do I Find Auditions?'

In a recent seminar Christopher Dietrich, the Executive Director of Actors Connection, said, "90% of actors get work without an agent. Even if you have an agent, don't sit back and wait for him to get you work. You should still be looking on your own."

There are plenty of books on *how* to audition, but only one other book (discussed below) that I have found which is dedicated to *finding* those auditions. Schools spend years teaching us how to act, but little, if any, attention is given to *where* actors can apply their hard learned skills. Sure, we see plays, movies, and television shows, but making it up to that screen or stage can seem like a million mile journey without a map. This guide was written to help direct you on your way.

Beginners will obviously learn the most from this book, but seasoned actors with and without representation will learn too.

You don't have to read the contents in order, but I recommend that you do as some topics discussed are expounded upon in later sections. Also, don't skip any section you may already be familiar with because you will most likely learn something new. Finally, for this print edition, eight casting directors and agents were nice enough to be interviewed, and I hope you find what they had to say as useful as I did.

Please email me with any questions, comments, suggestions, or success stories at **david@wheredoifindauditions.com**.

I should also add that while this book is not expressly about *how* to audition, that will be discussed a little, especially in the interview section. Same thing goes for how to find an agent.

What lies before you is years of knowledge accumulated through research, networking, and experience. Put that knowledge to work, get busy hustling, and you WILL find more auditions.

THE INTERNET

The web has been especially kind to actors. Not so long ago we had to "mail" headshots and resumes using "stamps" from these places called "post offices."*

Many, if not all, of you probably already use the web to submit to castings. Maybe you already have your own acting website. In this section I will introduce you to some new resources and show you a few ways to make better use of the ones you may already know.

I haven't included every single acting submission or resource website out there because how much time do we have...? Also, I've skipped some sites that seem to use questionable tactics like posting a breakdown on craigslist that leads to a pay site. Included are the ones that I have found beneficial and use the most. Since I live in New York, for example, I haven't included LA Castings, although I know a lot of LA casting directors *do* use it.

*in some cases, we still do.

Your Own Personal Website

Before we dive into the casting sites, let's talk a little about getting your own personal website.

Do it as soon as possible. After your headshot and resume, a webpage with strong content is probably your most versatile marketing tool. You can link to it in emails, and you should make the URL simple enough that if you send it on a postcard, agents or casting directors won't roll their eyes and throw up their hands if they try to type in the address.

Like a resume, there is no one correct format, but you absolutely should have your headshot on the homepage. Sounds like a no-brainer, but someone recently showed me his website, and there was an apple where a picture of his face should have been. Have a link to your resume and a link on that resume page to a printable copy of it. Have a link to a page of footage of good work that you've done. Have a link to a page with contact info for you and any representation you already have, even if you include some of this information already on the bottom of every page. Anything after that is gravy. I have a 'gallery' page which includes a couple of print jobs, onset photos, and a few more headshots. In fact, you can view my website at www.davidneallevin.com as an example. Search the web and you will find thousands more.

If you still feel a website is, at the moment, out of your reach, see the Now Casting section below.

But I don't know how to make a webpage...

Odds are you know someone who does. Talk to them and, hopefully, they will charge you a couple of hundred dollars or less or maybe even *nothing* to set it up depending on how well you know the person. A friend created mine, and I pay him $80/year for upkeep, and domain name renewal through GoDaddy.com which is $14.99/year. Given the number of casting directors that have said they enjoyed the videos on my site, it has been completely worth it.

If you are tech savvy or otherwise feeling adventurous, there are many make-your-own-website services available such as WordPress.com which is actually what my friend used to make mine.

I waited to create my website until I had an acting and commercial reel, but, in hindsight, I didn't need to do that. Headshot, resume, photos, and links to footage would have been a good start, and the reel could have been added later. So keep that in mind.

There is a lot more to be said about making your own website, but this should help give you some ideas to get started. It probably won't be easy, but it will definitely be worth it.

Actors Access – www.actorsaccess.com

Actors Access is the best self-submission site I know. "Self-submission" means that industry posts breakdowns, and you can submit yourself to them without needing an agent or manager. For those of you already signed up with Actors Access, hopefully you will learn a new "trick" or two here, and the rest of you should sign up right away.

After entering your profile for free, you can pay two dollars per submission or $68 for the year and submit as many times as you like. I submit to at least several breakdowns a week or more, so the yearly fee makes sense for me, but pay-by-breakdown if you're tentative (although you shouldn't be).

Breakdowns can include union and non-union commercials, theater, movies, web series, television, and more. You probably won't find too many union principal roles for "big budget" national commercials, movies, or network television listed, but it does happen. Several years ago I saw a listing for a film entitled *A Serious Man* to be directed by someone with the last name 'Coen'.

"Huh," I thought, "there's another director out there with the last name Coen," and submitted without thinking twice. Before I knew it, I was auditioning for a Coen brothers' movie. Wow! The role wound up going to Richard Kind, but wow.

Not so long ago I saw a breakdown for LINCOLN of *Abraham Lincoln: Vampire Hunter* fame. So while most roles you see might not have quite that high a profile, they do pop up from time to time.

Great, so how do I get this ball rolling?

Entering your profile online is pretty easy and self–explanatory. You have to input your resume line by line which can take some time, but that is typical of most self-submission sites. You can also upload up to two headshots or other photos for free and later replace those with new photos at no extra charge. Each photo you have on your profile in addition to the first two costs $10.

You can also upload a reel or "performance video" for $22/minute worth of footage for casting directors to see, but if you already have your reel online or a personal webpage, you can usually include the web address in the submission notes (more on that later). One advantage of going the "performance video" route is that your submission will appear to casting directors before submissions that don't have a performance video. That's not always the case, however, as Actors Access General Manager Bob Brody explains:

> "Yes, submissions with Performance Video are listed before submissions without video. But that is the default. Casting has the ability to arrange submissions as they please via sort filters such as alphabetically by last name, date time, etc. If for instance actor Joe Zebra submits with a Performance Video and actor Sam Able submits without, Joe Zebra's submission will be listed before Sam Able's. That's the default. But if casting sorts by name instead, Sam Able will come before Joe Zebra regardless that Joe has video included."

I did not initially go the performance video route as I thought having my website in the submission notes would be sufficient. But after seeing that *Jimmy Kimmel Live* was only considering profiles with reels for the week the show was shooting in Brooklyn, I started considering it. It wasn't until manager Nicole Astell recommended doing it that finally bit the bullet. I have not gotten an audition from Actors Access by including my performance reel with submission since. Make of that what you will.

Breakdowns

Under 'my tools' and then 'my account' make sure there is a check next to:

"Notify me by e-mail when a project is released that contains one or more roles that match my profile."

Actors Access usually sends me three or four emails per day during the week with anywhere from one to twenty breakdowns each (I think the most I've ever received is thirty). Their filter is very good as I cannot recall ever receiving a breakdown for a female or some other type of role that clearly did not match my profile. Just click on the breakdown in the email, and you will be taken to the login for the site. To save a little time, especially on a smart phone, leave the breakdown page you are viewing open even if you decided not to submit to it so you don't have to login multiple times to view more than one breakdown from the same email.

At the end of every day or so, I double-check the breakdowns on the site itself in case there's something that slipped through or that I missed the first time around. Click on 'Breakdowns' in the top row and select the city you want to search. It will return all breakdowns for that city and as a SAG-AFTRA member I usually select the "Union breakdowns fit for me" filter and search those results. There are other filters so make sure to select the one best for you. Breakdowns to which you've already submitted will have a checkmark by them.

Submitting - "Oh boy, here goes nothing!!!"

Whoa, easy, pardner! Here are some important things to keep in mind before submitting:

Double-check the breakdown's audition, callback, and shoot dates before submitting to make sure you can make them all. If you want to see an unhappy casting director, get booked for a role and then tell them you can't make the shoot.

Don't submit for every breakdown that matches your profile. Only submit for roles that match your type, or you will drive casting directors insane. What's your "type"? There are people who help actors figure that out for a living, but briefly: Did you see my headshot? I am not submitting for handsome leading man roles. Yes, my mom thinks I'm handsome (and she's not wrong), but in the casting world I am more of the next door neighbor, office guy, kinda creepy, weirdo type. I've played other things, of course, but I hope you get what I'm saying.

After you click on the role you want to submit for and are directed to the page to pick the photo you want to send, you will usually see a place at the bottom to leave a note for the casting director. Only do this if you have something really relevant to say. For example, if the breakdown states that they are looking for actors with comedic improv skills, I will add the note, "I have over 8 years improv performance experience" because sometimes it's hard to tell from a resume how long an actor's been doing a thing.

If you have a link to an online reel or webpage, the submission note is a good place to paste it. I usually write, "You can view my reels at www.davidneallevin.com". I would also recommend putting your website in your Actors Access resume notes in case there isn't a notes section in the breakdown so maybe the casting director will see it there. Sometimes the breakdown will specifically ask you something like "Please note your archery experience in your submission," but keep it to one or two sentences at most.

SUMMARY

I did not book a single thing my first year on Actors Access, possibly due to my fledgling audition skills, but I am glad I stuck with it. Unless you have commercial and legit agents sending you out A LOT, I think every actor should have an account with Actors Access. Sometimes casting directors for television use Showfax for posting audition sides, and if you are registered with Actors Access you can peruse them for free. That's where I had to download sides for my one *Nurse Jackie* audition and a pilot for Denis Leary's production company. The point is, sign up!!!

- Enter your profile FREE and then pay as you go or annually. Do the annual one.

- Make sure you checked to receive emails with breakdowns matching your profile.

- Check breakdowns on website itself every day or so in case something slipped through.

- Only add relevant info to submission notes like links to reels or requested experience.

Craigslist – www.craigslist.org

Some of you may be thinking, "I check craigslist sometimes, and there's not much there," or "I don't want to be in a tickle video." Despite craigslist's seedy reputation, there ARE many legitimate, non-porn acting gigs to be found.

Several years ago I almost gave up on craigslist. It was a Wednesday night, and I thought, "Jeez, what am I wasting my time slumming on here for?" I could feel my soul shrinking. But I decided to give craigslist ONE. MORE. TRY. I checked the "tv/film/video" jobs section and found recent postings for two auditions: one for a marketing company and one for a new administrative healthcare device. I applied to both, and both called me in for auditions that Friday. As it happened, I wound up booking both gigs; a great day. The healthcare audition was pretty laid back: script guided improv* in front of a couple of people in an office in Chinatown. After I did my thing, they reminded me that the rate was $50, and then asked, "Do you think that's too low?"

"Well, maybe it's a *little* low, but not too, too low."

After I did the gig which took less than an hour, they gave me a check for $100. Not a ton of money but still *double* their initial rate and not bad for an hour's work. Keep in mind that it's usually only small productions that will pay you the same day because they don't have a huge bureaucracy through which to funnel your money.

The marketing company audition was also heavily improvised off of a script. The project featured 'wacky' characters having an insult or "slam" competition for an internal video for their software company client. My character was a Russian gymnastics coach encouraging his protegé. The rate was $250/day for one day's work. The first day we all arrived at the marketing office in Tribeca early in the morning and sat around until mid-afternoon when the producers admitted that they still had a lot of set-up to do, and we'd have to reschedule, BUT we'd still be paid for the day. The new call time was 7 a.m. on a Saturday. When I arrived, one of the producers told me that too many people had cancelled for the day, and we'd have to reschedule again, BUT we'd still be paid for the day. Great, so far $500 dollars, and all I've had to do is show up. The third day they finally had their act together. We finished shooting everything, and they told us we'd get paid within two weeks. Unfortunately, the client was late in paying the producers, so it took closer to a month. It didn't really bother me, but I know some of the other actors had complained about the delay. So when I

14

went to pick up my check and the producer started to write out the amount, I could see her hand hesitate and instead of writing a check for $750, she made it out for $800, possibly because I had been polite and patient about the whole thing, unlike some of the other actors, or maybe she felt bad about the delay or both.

So, because I decided to give craigslist "ONE. MORE. TRY." I made $900 from acting work. Obviously a day like that is rare, but I have since been checking craigslist five nights a week and have made over two thousand dollars from non-porn acting work.

"Five nights a week? That's a lot!"

Make it a chore; make it a habit; make it a part of your career.

Check at least Monday through Friday because, occasionally, there are posts for jobs happening the NEXT DAY. Once I saw a union AFTRA post for the PBS science show *NOVA* that was auditioning the next morning. I submitted, thinking surely they would call on such short notice to schedule an audition. Instead they sent an email I didn't see until noon the next day by which time it was too late. So, if you've submitted, start checking your email as soon as you can the next morning. Even if a post is for an audition happening in two or three days, if you miss that first day to submit, they will probably fill up audition slots before you can respond.

On weekends there are fewer postings so don't feel too bad if you are out of town or otherwise internet-less. Just remember to check Sunday night or whenever you return.

"So where do I find auditions on this craigslist?"

As I've already mentioned, there is the 'tv/film/video' section under the 'jobs' column to the right of the page. I found the marketing and healthcare device gigs here among other auditions. You will also find non-acting jobs here related to the industry. There are usually not an overwhelming number of postings here, so scanning today's posts and clicking on what sounds relevant to you should not take much time.

The other place to check is under the 'gigs' heading in the 'talent' section. There can be well over a hundred new postings a day in this section which can be a little intimidating, but if you use the 'search for' feature, you will save yourself a lot of time and find auditions you might otherwise have missed.

So what should I 'search for'?

First decide if you want to find gigs that are 'pay', 'no-pay', or 'all' (meaning your search will include both 'pay' and 'non-pay' gigs), and click on the appropriate button under the 'search for' field. When I first started out and was still looking for footage for my reel, I would select 'all' in case a 'no-pay' project came up that looked like it might yield some good footage. For example, I applied and booked a student film as a jerky club manager, something I don't often get to play. Now I usually only search under 'pay' gigs, but if you are still looking for footage for your reel or simply looking for experience and to make contacts, you might want to select 'all'.

Next, think about what words you'll 'search for' that will narrow down the field. What skills do you have that a producer/director/casting director might be looking for? Guitar, juggling, martial arts? What types of gigs are you looking for? Comedy, drama, commercial? What physical traits do you possess that make you stand out? Plus size, blonde, goatee?

To give you a better idea of what I mean, let's break *me* down into search terms. I'm bald on top, so I'd want a search that included the words 'bald, 'balding', 'receding', 'receded', and 'thinning'. Sounds like a lot, but different people use different words to describe the same thing. When I had a beard, I found a job that only came up because I'd searched for the word 'bearded'. 'Beard' and 'beards' did not bring up that job post on a search. I wound up booking the job and it paid $300 for a day's work, a job I would not have found had I not searched using the word 'bearded'. Okay, what else about me? I have a mustache, so I'll search for 'mustache', 'mustaches', 'moustache', and 'moustaches'. I used to search for 'moustachioed' but that eventually felt kind of ridiculous (who knows what I have missed out on as a result!). Also depending on the current lunar cycle, I am 'chubby'. And, lest I forget, ladies, I can also do 'creepy'.

What skills do I have? Well, I'm pretty good at improv, and improv is 'hot' right now, so I'll search for the words 'improv', 'improviser', 'improvisers', 'improvisor', and 'improvisors'. I'm also pretty 'funny' and occasionally 'hilarious'.

What kind of work am I most interested in? "Comedy," so I'll search for comedy, comic, comics, comedic, comedian, and comedians.

Finally, just to cover my bases, I'll search for 'male', 'males', 'actor', and 'actors'.

Here's the list all lumped together:

Bald, balding, receding, receded, thinning, mustache, mustaches, moustache, moustaches, chubby, creepy, improv, improviser, improvisers, , improvisor, improvisors, funny, hilarious, comedy, comic, comics, comedic, comedian, comedians, male, males, actor, and actors.
That's 28 searches, five days a week for several years.

"That will take forever!"

Make it a part of your daily routine. There will be many nights when you are tired and want to skip it, but what does that say about your drive to be an actor? This is part of the 'hustle' on your way to becoming a working actor. It only took me 5-15 minutes a day, depending on how many auditions I found and submitted for. Then my friend Rocco Privetera showed me a faster, easier way to search that I will now pass on to you.

Once you've figured out your search terms, you can enter them all at once in the 'search for' field as a string. Then bookmark that page so every time you open it, the search is automatically done for you.
Here's what a search string would look like with my terms in it:

improv* | bald* | comed* | comic* | funny | hilarious | male* | actor* | reced* | moustach* | mustach* | creepy | chubby

Notice that you can truncate words and put an asterisk at the end of them to search for terms that contain those first few letters and anything that comes after them. For example, entering 'improv*'(don't use the quotation marks) will return searches for 'improv', 'improviser', 'improvisers', 'improvisor', and 'improvisors'. The character between the words is called a 'pipe' and will most likely be located on the same key as the backslash on your keyboard.

Rocco just saved us about 10 minutes a day or almost two full days a year. Thanks, Rocco!

I'd recommend looking at posts from no more than five days previous since anything posted before that has probably already been cast. Once you start searching on a regular basis, you'll notice the links to the posts you've already clicked on are a different color (probably purple) so you know you don't have to go back much farther in time than that.

"How do I know this ad is for real?"

Most jobs I've found are legitimate, by which I mean 'not fake'. But if a job listing sounds too good to be true, then it probably is. Major motion pictures (not including indies) and television shows will almost never post for roles, even roles for extras, on craigslist. They pay money to casting directors for that. Avoid anyone you contact that wants money upfront unless it's for a workshop or class, and, even then, you might want to Google them to be safe. Agents will never post ads looking for new clients, and if they do, consider saving yourself for an agent with a little more clout.

If an ad seems a little off or you're just not sure about it, treat it like a blind date. Research them or ask as many questions as you need to make yourself feel comfortable before meeting them. No audition is worth your safety and well-being.

"Found an audition! Now what?"

Unless they ask for a cover letter or want to know "Why do you think you'd be perfect for this role?" which rarely happens, I'd stick to the 'less is more' reply philosophy. They are most likely going to pay the most attention to your headshot and resume, not your email note. Here's the reply format I use:

Hi[if a contact name is listed use that],

I saw your post on craigslist and have attached my headshot and resume for your consideration[if they listed more than one role, say the role/s you are applying for. For example, "…for your consideration of the role of HENRY." If no specific role is listed or it is for only one role, just end with "for your consideration."]. You can view my reels at www.davidneallevin.com [of course, skip this if you don't have a website or reel. If you do, make it a link.]

Thanks,
David
[even though it's on the resume, I also put my phone number under my name to make it easier for them to contact me.]

And that's it! They have everything they need to know. No need to go on and on about how much you've been inspired by *Downton Abbey*.

If they mention they are looking for a specific skill, you should mention that you do, in fact, have that skill and how much experience you have in it. For example, if a post is looking for someone with an improv background/experience, I'll add, "I have almost 8 years of improv performance experience." There, done.

Once you start applying for these auditions, you will save a lot of time by going to your email 'Sent' box, finding the last audition email you sent out, changing the relevant information such as email, role, possible contact name (double check to avoid embarrassment!), and then forwarding that 'old' email along to your new contact.

SUMMARY

People do look for actors for real non-skeevy work on craigslist. Maybe not for major motion pictures or union television shows, but you will find lots of non-union work. Like I said, by checking only a few minutes a day, I've made over two thousand dollars from acting work found on craigslist. Yes, the occasional questionable post pops up, but you have the power to ignore it. So remember:

- Check Sunday through Friday, or even more often if you feel up to it.

- Check 'tv/film/video' in the 'jobs' section.

- Check 'talent' under the 'gigs' section.

- Create a search string you can bookmark and to save you time.

- Keep your replies to posts brief.

- Better safe than sorry!

<u>Backstage</u> - www.backstage.com

Backstage is a publication filled with articles, interviews, columns, breakdowns, and many other useful actor things. It is an excellent resource, and many of its features are available on the web for FREE. Access to their castings, however, does cost money: $144/year as of this writing (if you pay the year in advance; monthly is more expensive), making it the most expensive subscription service listed here.

Is it worth it?

Several years ago I had an online subscription and booked a couple of low paying non-union jobs from it (one of which contacted me directly after seeing my headshot on the *Backstage* site, so that can happen) and several other auditions. At the end of the year, the subscription didn't exactly pay for itself, and because of the relatively high cost, I didn't renew. But after letting the subscription lapse, I continued to receive casting emails from *Backstage*, and when I clicked through some of them, the contact info was available before the listing was abruptly cut-off. If I had renewed, I could have read the entire breakdown, but for many of them I didn't need to read the whole breakdown to submit, so why bother paying another $144? After about six months the breakdowns stopped coming, but because of the relatively high price, I still didn't bother renewing.

Now I wish I had. There are a lot of breakdowns on *Backstage*, many of them non-union, and who knows what I might have found in those several years before I had to join SAG-AFTRA. So I would recommend giving it a try.

Well, why don't you rejoin now?

Most of the union posts that come up for me when I search now are for theater. When I'm feeling ready to audition for stage again, I probably will.

In the meantime…

Like I said, many of the great things about *Backstage* (aside from castings) can be found online for FREE. There are tons of informative advice columns, interviews, articles, and reviews in their newsletter 'Backstage Espresso' which you can subscribe to for FREE here: www.backstage.com/newsletter/

My favorite advice columns are 'Secret Agent Man' where an anonymous but real Hollywood Legit Agent doles out knowledge and 'The Working Actor' where working actor Michael Kostroff (you may know him best from *The Wire*) answers readers' letters (although he currently seems to be on hiatus).

The message board is also a great resource: http://bbs.backstage.com/groupee

Just start browsing *Backstage* online and you will find a lot of good information.

SUMMARY

• If you are still non-union and can afford it, you should try *Backstage*.

• Subscribe FREE to 'Backstage Espresso': http://www.backstage.com/newsletter/

• You could spend hours browsing this website!

Playbill – www.playbill.com

You know those booklets they hand out at shows that some people collect that say 'Playbill' on them? Well, *Playbill* has a website.

In addition to articles on what's happening in the theater world, *Playbill* also has a 'Job Listings' link about halfway down the column on the left-hand side of their home page. Here it is: www.playbill.com/jobs/find/

As you might expect, the majority of listings are for theater gigs in New York, but some are for gigs, jobs, and internships in the entertainment industry in New York and beyond. You can also narrow your search using the fields at the bottom of the listings by category, state, keyword, and date posted. Usually I don't use the search fields since I conveniently live in New York and *Playbill* usually only posts about one to two new pages of listings per day; so eyeballing the new listings is not as taxing as it might be on, say, craigslist. The listings are updated Monday through Friday, so I'd encourage you to check them every weeknight.

Playbill online also has a ton of information on the latest theater news, so it is an all-around great free resource.

SUMMARY

- View **FREE** job listings.

- Check it Monday through Friday.

Casting Networks – www.castingnetworks.com

Casting Networks is a database of talent which industry can and does search to find actors for their projects. It is similar to Actors Access in that it also has many breakdowns to which talent can self-submit. There are not a lot of parts for BIG movies or television shows aside from extra roles, but there are many non-union productions and commercials listed. In fact, I once ran into someone who took my workshop who said he went in earlier that day for an audition for a non-union *Comedy Central* promo he found on Casting Networks.

On any given day, under the 'Principal Roles' section on my homepage, Casting Networks has today posted two commercials, two print jobs, five student projects, one short film and four live events that match my profile criteria, all of which, I should add, are non-union. Under the 'Extras Roles' section it has listed 39 breakdowns posted for the day, and it may be only 2 p.m. During most weeks I easily get that many emails or *more* to sift through every day for extra roles in New York. It can be a bit overwhelming. An acting acquaintance once asked me about finding extra work, and I told him about Casting Networks.

He said, "Yeah, but they send out so many emails, I just turned the email option off."

How badly could he have wanted acting work since he wasn't willing to sift through some emails to find it?

There is, however, an option in your profile to receive only Principal Role notifications via email if you are not interested in extra work. I like receiving the extra role notifications because sometimes I have nothing to do the next day and might want to try to get some extra work. Plus, it's a convenient way of finding out what television shows and movies are currently shooting in your area.

I should mention that I have the non-union email option deselected, and yet I'm still getting non-union breakdowns. What's up with that, Casting Networks? I emailed to ask them and received no reply.

Okay, they so have breakdowns, what else?

When you start working with an agent, he or she will most likely have you setup a Casting Networks profile so he can more easily submit you to some breakdowns. Also, more and more casting offices are using Casting

Networks as a way for you to check-in at auditions. Instead of them having to take your photo and fill out a size card every time you show up for an audition, you can simply log-in to Casting Networks and the casting directors receive the info they need. You should still have your wardrobe sizes memorized and a headshot/resume with you just in case.

Does industry *really* contact you directly through this site for work?

Yes! As you will read in the interviews below, casting directors do, in fact, use Casting Networks. Once I was contacted about being a stand-in for Louis C.K. for his show *Louie*. Over the course of several days, they had me email a bunch of shots of my head from many different angles, and finally, I was told, "Okay, they *might* need you, but won't know until 7 a.m. the day of the shoot. So wait to see if they call you." They did not call, but they did initially find me on Casting Networks.

So how much is all of this going to cost me?

All of the fun above can be yours for only five dollars a month. They do have other premium services like having the ability to post videos and such which do cost extra. In fact, it is a little annoying that unlike, Actors Access, Casting Networks does NOT let you post in the optional submission note anything that remotely looks like it could lead to your webpage or reel when you submit for a role. Instead, they have a "media hosting" option for $5 extra per month that allows you to upload unlimited clips that can be up to 4 minutes long. They want that money, and I'm actually considering that clip option.

SUMMARY

- Daily emails of Principal (mostly non-union) and MANY Extra (union and non-union) breakdowns

- Used by industry to find talent (found me once, sort of!) and facilitate auditions

- $5 per month for basic subscription

Jagger's List – www.castingsnclasses.com

Jagger Kaye is a working actor in New York who started an acting community in 2004 with an email list offering castings, classes, and other events including some for charity. His website claims it sends out over 4,500 castings a year and that is not hard to believe. One day, I received over forty emails from his list. Some days there are fewer, some days more, and some days there are none, depending on how Jagger is feeling, but forty is not that surprising. To give you some idea of what's in all of these emails, at least half of one day's emails are for castings, then some are emails for new classes, and some are announcements. There is a wide variety of castings both union and non-union for theater, student films and independent projects to name a few. I've only seen a couple of the castings posted elsewhere so it is definitely, for me at least, a source of new information. People also email Jagger asking him to post castings, location searches, etc. for their own projects and he does (otherwise, how would I know?) which is awfully nice of him. One recent email was a forwarded request from a woman looking for a house in which to shoot a short film. If you're intimidated by all of these emails, again ask yourself how many emails you are willing to read in the pursuit of your acting career.

As I mentioned, Jagger also offers many different types of classes and they are generally pretty inexpensive. A sampling: one night Commercial Industry event with casting director David Vaccari of Telsey - $42.50; one day Commercial Intensive with Jagger - $50; four week Improv Class with "mini-show" with agent Jerry Kallarakkal of DDO - $149.50; and one night Voiceover Industry event with agent Robert Slavin of Buchwald - $38.50. I have only taken one of Jagger's classes, the 'Auditioning for the Agent' Class with Jerry Kallarakkal of DDO for $48.50. I came into the class with three questions and left with only two of them answered because during the one-on-one portion of the session, I spent too much time talking improv with Jerry and didn't hear the one minute warning knock at the door so mea culpa. But I would take the class again and recommend it, especially for the chance to pick an agent's brain at that price. I can't personally vouch for any of the other classes, but the website says that Jagger's classes are "the Backstage Readers Choice Awards Record Holder for Most Mentions in History, Twenty-six", so make of that what you will.

Great, so how do I get on this magical mailing list?

To add more emails to your life, you must join Jagger's Yahoo group which currently has over 13,000 members: http://groups.yahoo.com/group/CnC-CASTINGS/

When I joined I remember it taking ten minutes of hunting around for links, but it looks like things have been simplified. If not, you have been warned.

SUMMARY

Yes, it can be a lot of emails, but again, how many emails are you willing to go through to find work?

- FREE to sign up

- LOTS of castings, of which, I'd unscientifically say about half are for theater

- Inexpensive classes, at least one of which I can recommend

Now Casting – www.nowcasting.com

Now Casting is a free website that has breakdowns and, like Actors Access, lets you manually input your credits and upload your headshot onto a profile page that you will use for submissions. You can also list links for FREE on your profile to reels on youtube, or, better yet, your own website. Now Casting also lets you use their webpage as a 'personal' web destination for people to view your credits and headshot, etc. with an address something like http://davidneallevin.nowcasting.com. This may not be a bad stop-gap until you get your own url.

If you upgrade your Now Casting membership with *money*, you can upload reels and clips directly onto your profile (but if you can list links to footage on your profile for free, then why I do that?). They also have other services like making your website fancier for a monthly fee. I have never tried any of these 'upgrades' since they have my basic information and they allow me to submit free.

So why am I here again?

Now Casting does have a lot of breakdowns, most of which seem to be non-union. In fact, I'm looking at 'Notices Fit for Me' right now and they are all non-union. I even have union checked on my profile and I'm still getting these. Notices do seem to be mostly determined by your profile details, but, occasionally, under 'Notices Fit for Me' I'll see breakdowns looking for blondes, females, Asians, and other things this brown haired, white boy is not. It makes me wonder what's on the 'Notices NOT Fit for Me' page, and for the first time ever, dear reader, I am going to look... it says, and I am not joking, "Sorry, no projects available!" Obviously, something seems to be amiss.

I have been called in for two auditions from Now Casting notices: one was for a music video, and the other was for an indie movie *The Golden Scallop* which I wound up booking and was one of the best experiences of my life. Still, two auditions over 4-5 years is not that great, so I only log in about once a week these days to see what's now... casting. Once, maybe twice a week, I'll receive an email with a breakdown or two from them which is thoughtful, but I feel it's as if they're saying, "Hey, remember us! Come visit!"

So *WHY* am I here again?

It may sound like I've been bashing Now Casting, but I like it, quirks and all, because if you are non-union, there are a ton of breakdowns. I've even seen breakdowns for Tyler Perry movies listed on Now Casting although not so much lately. As I look now under current 'All Casting Notices' I see non-union breakdowns under the categories of Television, Feature Film, Commercial & Industrials, Stage/Variety, Shorts & Student Projects, and Reality TV/Game Show. The one union notice is for a student film in California. None are for established high profile projects, but there might be one day.

Now Casting also emails out a decent weekly newsletter called 'Actors Ink' which has articles by working actors and industry professionals with titles like *Audition Strategy #32* and *Feeling Stuck in Your Acting Career? 7 Steps to Set you Free*. Generally these are not as good as Backstage articles, but they are free, and they are only trying to help (and possibly sell you on a class).

SUMMARY

- FREE

- Can build an acting website of sorts

- Lots of non-union breakdowns

- Free newsletter

- Check at least several times a week

<u>Scott Powers Studios</u> - www.scottpowers.com

The charming and dapper Scott Powers offers classes, seminars, and more at his Midtown studio. Full disclosure: I have never taken one. Once I met an actor at a cattle-call who said he had taken one of Scott's classes, and he started working with an agent as a result; so there's a third party endorsement for you. Years ago I almost attended a meet-and-greet at the studio that listed among its many participants someone who had worked on *Arrested Development*, and the ad had an accompanying image of the FOX sitcom to promote it. Then a friend pointed out to me that the guest had *actually* worked on an independent project that happened to have the same name. Let's chalk that up to an honest mistake.

So why I am here?

What I really like about Scott Powers Studios is their mailing list. Once, sometimes even twice a week, Scott emails out a 'Weekly Tip'. Recent selections include 'Rules of the Business', 'Taking Direction', and 'Background Work – Part 1'. And they're usually pretty good! Some are practical, some are motivational and some are both. I always read them because even if I don't learn something new, they are a nice shot in the arm to keep hustling.

Even better than the weekly tips, however, are the emails announcing a **FREE Friday Lunch Bunch**. Every week or so, Scott has industry guests (agents, managers, directors, casting directors) come in for you to meet in a group setting and ask questions for FREE. He even provides refreshments or "lunch" like pizza, sandwiches, or cold-cuts. You have to call-in the Wednesday before to reserve your place, but I've never had a problem with this. At the Lunch Bunch, you and about 19 other actors sit in a semi-circle chatting with Scott about classes and whatever for around 30 minutes, and then the guest arrives to tell you about themselves, what they do, and finally take your questions. Afterwards, they collect your headshot and resume because maybe you're a segment of that semi-circle they'll want to meet with later. At one Lunch Bunch I attended, a guest cancelled last minute but wound up calling in all of the attendees to read some commercial copy for her. Thoughtful! I've been to about half-a-dozen of these and have never been contacted by a guest later. But don't let that discourage you. Odds are you're probably not going to hear back from the majority of industry you meet, even the ones for which you audition.

So how do I stand out amongst all these semi-circled-up actors?

Ask the guest a sincere and intelligent question. This is a low pressure and FREE opportunity to pick the brain of industry. Think in advance about something you'd want to ask them. That way even if they never call you, at least you'll have the answer to a burning question or two.

Also make sure the resume and headshot you are presenting is up-to-date. Headshots that don't look like you or poorly formatted resumes with too much filler can be signs that the person on the other end is an amateur.

Here's a personal lesson in what NOT to do:

During one of the last Lunch Bunch's I attended, the agent mentioned that he loved history. I love history, too. But raising my hand and saying, "Hey, we should work together because I minored in history in college!" did not sound sane. I fretted with the frustration of the socially awkward and non-telepathic. A little later he said that he loved Wonder Woman. I don't love Wonder Woman, but I happened to have in my bag a Wonder Woman button I'd been carrying around to give to a friend. I was sure this friend would understand. When it came time to pass in our headshots/resumes, I perforated them both with that Wonder Woman button, and wrote a note that I'm *sure* did not sound like I was a stalker. If you've been reading carefully, you'll already know how this ended.

Join Scott's mailing list on his website. You can find the link at the top of his home page.

Yes, some emails are ads for classes and seminars, but Scott doesn't flood you with them. I've never looked at my inbox and thought, "ANOTHER class from this place?"

Occasionally Scott will send out casting breakdowns as well.

SUMMARY

I cannot personally vouch for the classes, but definitely get on Scott's mailing list.

- Weekly Tips

- FREE Friday Lunch Bunch with industry

- Occasional breakdowns

- Save your buttons for your friends.

<u>Mandy's</u> – www.mandy.com

Mandy's is a Film and TV Production Directory with categories for services, jobs, castings, film markets, and classifieds to name most of them. You're probably most concerned with 'castings'.

Mandy seems to have mostly student and low budget/non-paying posts for castings so these days I tend not to search there very often. In fact, I just did a search for 'fully paid' positions for ANY gender, ethnicity, age range, production type or union affiliation, and only seven postings were listed in the New York area. I then tried the same thing with 'Paid + lo/no' (meaning low or no pay in addition to paid gigs), and twenty listings came back. Still not a lot for the New York area. This has been my general Mandy searching experience. I almost gave up on Mandy altogether a few years ago until I met someone outside the Magnet Theater who had come from an NYU print shoot.

"Oh, where did you find out about that project?" I asked.

"Mandy's"

"Really... *Mandy's*...?"

So I still check, periodically, JUST IN CASE. And although I have never gotten an audition from this website, your experience may be different.

Mandy also allows you to upload your headshot and resume for free. However I tried to edit my resume a while ago, and it kept asking me to log-in (even though I had done so correctly) again, again, and again. You might have to try another computer to log-in successfully.

Mandy does seem to have a lot more listings for other industry jobs, covering all aspects of production. In fact, one of the cameramen in the last indie feature I worked on said he regularly looked for and found work on Mandy's. So tell your pre-, post-, and production friends.

SUMMARY

• FREE

• I have not had much luck here, but others have.

- Tell your production friends about the 'jobs' section.

- Check more often than I do.

Impossible Casting – www.impossiblecasting.com

Impossible Casting is a (SURPRISE!) casting agency that, in addition to handling castings for what might be considered more 'mainstream' roles, also handles what might be considered 'hard-to-cast' or 'impossible' roles. A recent search returned these breakdowns: MALE/AF AMER / 25-40, BEARD AND MUSTACHE, stand in for Wyatt Cenac, 6ft tall thin build; MALE/FEMALE/ ANY AGE: VERY tattooed hand and arm; and FEMALE 18-40, BODY BUILDERS, people with MASSIVE physiques. Not exactly impossible, but maybe a little different from what you might be used to seeing. And there are other breakdowns too.

I have tattoos on my big muscles! Where do I sign up?

Team Impossible has a FREE mailing list that sends out breakdowns several times a week on average. Over the years I've responded to maybe a dozen breakdowns I thought were appropriate for me and have only been called in for a few, but one of those was for an Absolut print ad I wound up booking, so no complaints!

Impossible's list also promotes showcases and seminars with industry guests, but these plugs almost always accompany a casting they are looking to fill. I attended one of their seminars where I read for a prominent casting director whom I've awkwardly run into several times since. But I'm glad I went. Their office also features late 20th century posters and toys. Remember the 20th century, kids?

Okay, so...

You can sign up for the Impossible Casting mailing list in the field next to the 'subscribe' button here:
http://www.impossiblecasting.com/actorindex.htm

Sometimes you might see some of their breakdowns on other sites like Actors Access or Casting Networks after you've see them on the mailing list, but that only means they are casting a wider net because some of those castings are nigh impossible.

SUMMARY

- FREE mailing list that sends the breakdowns to YOU

- office filled with radical pop-culture nostalgia

Casting Frontier – www.castingfrontier.com

Casting Frontier is similar to many other websites in that you can input your profile (headshot, resume) and submit yourself to breakdowns. They also, occasionally, email out breakdowns, probably the least frequently of any website that emails out breakdowns listed here.

Entering your basic profile is free and so is submitting. For people in LA, there are a fair amount of breakdowns listed, mostly non-union. Recently there were 39 unsorted LA breakdowns that had been listed over a four day period, three of which were union. If you live in NY like me, however, there are only five breakdowns listed; the most recent of which was posted almost a month ago. Not so great. Keep in mind that this is the most unscientific of samplings. If you stick with the free profile listing, you have nothing to lose.

So, why am I here?

Some casting houses use Casting Frontier instead of Casting Networks to check you in at auditions. Most notably in New York is Beth Melsky Casting which is a big one and actually the only one, as far as my email can tell; when you check in using Frontier and Networks, they send you an email confirming you did so. It's worth spending the thirty minutes or so to fill out your free Casting Frontier profile if, for no other reason, that one day Melsky might call you in for an audition.

SUMMARY

- Entering basic online profile is FREE

- Some breakdowns, mostly non-union, mostly in LA

- Certain casting houses use the site for your check in; sign up so you'll be ready.

Improv Resource Center - www.improvresourcecenter.com

The Improv Resource Center (IRC) is a message board ostensibly for improvisers, but anyone can use it. It's popularity has waned somewhat in recent years with the rise of Facebook but I still think it is worth checking out. The IRC has threads on jobs, apartments, performance spaces, and of course, improv shows. Locations featured are New York, LA, Philadelphia, D.C., Chicago, North Carolina, Arizona, and Other Places. Some cities have more posts than others with New York currently having the most.

You can browse without having a login, but to post or reply to a post you need an account which is free (unless someone has included a reply email in the post for you to use).

People post all kinds of things, and some of them are looking for like-minded comedians to do projects with. You might not find many paid gigs, but it is a place to connect with people who are looking to do creative things, and who knows where that could lead.

The major improv theaters in New York City also have their own message boards or forums:

Upright Citizens Bridage http://boards.ucbcomedy.com/index.php

Magnet Theater http://www.magnettheater.com/community/index.php

The PIT used to have a great forum that was dropped for some reason from their new website.

Search for the comedy community's message board in your hometown, and surround yourself with positive, creative people.

SUMMARY

- Find the comedy message boards in your community.

<u>Theatrical Index</u> – www.theatricalindex.com

Confession time: I first heard of this website after reading Erica Palgon's interview (see below), and, therefore, am not that familiar with it. But if it's good enough for Erica, it is worth mentioning here.

'Theatrical Index' is, according to its website, an up-to-date, publication of "all the shows on Broadway, Off-Broadway, Touring Productions, and the Premieres across the country."

If you are interested in theater, try the one-week trial. You can contact directors of upcoming productions, and, if you do so deftly enough, they might just grant you an audition. More about that in Brian O'Neil's book which is discussed below.

<u>Telsey Youtube Project</u>

In case you're interested in Musicals, Telsey and Company in NYC has a video submission form where you can submit an audition for projects. Long shot? You bet! But they do say someone will watch it, and if you don't have an agent or other way to get submitted for something you think you can nail, then why not try? This is the web address: http://www.telseyandco.com/contact-2/8-uncategorised/16-telsey-company-youtube-project

FINAL THOUGHTS

There are SO many resources and castings on the internet that it can be easy to get overwhelmed. Don't be. Remember your commitment to being and find work as an actor. Make checking these sites a part of your routine, a part of your job, because it is! Until the day you become so sought after that you can pick and choose your projects. In the meantime, you don't want to miss an opportunity because you neglected to find it.

MEET & GREETS:
WORKSHOPS, CLASSES, and SEMINARS

Hopefully, you have already taken many scene study, acting, and technique classes, and will continue to do so to perfect your craft. By the way, if you are having trouble finding the right one for you, read this *Backstage* article for some helpful tips:

http://www.backstage.com/advice-for-actors/backstage-experts/4-things-consider-when-finding-acting-teacher/

In this section I'm referring to the short-term, one to three night acting workshops/classes where you go to meet and, essentially, audition for casting directors or other industry, and, hopefully, learn a few things. Usually you receive sides in advance (typically a short scene the instructor has worked with before), and then perform in front of the class, taking adjustments/direction from the instructor. At the beginning or end of the class there is usually a Q&A. These type of workshops generally cost around $100-200.

There are also shorter and usually less expensive sessions where you meet and perform a monologue or sides for an agent or director or casting director and then briefly talk or "meet" with them. These are colloquially called 'meet and greets', and they generally cost anywhere from $25-60.

Are these workshops and 'meet and greets' worth it?

They can be if you are prepared and do some research in advance. But before getting into that, let me discuss some classes and venues for classes in the New York City area that are probably similar to places in your area (especially if you live in NY or LA).

Brooke and Mary – www.brookeandmary.com

If you live in the NYC area and are at all interested in auditioning for commercials, you should take a class from Brooke Thomas and Mary Callahan. Both have worked as casting directors at House Productions. Brooke (interviewed in the next section) recently left to start Brooke Thomas Casting, but they both still join forces to teach their popular class.

For three nights over three weeks you learn commercial audition techniques, apply them to copy, get feedback, and in the final class perform the copy of your choice for two commercial agents. So in addition to learning how to become better at auditioning for commercials, you also get to get to know and 'audition' for two casting directors (Brooke and Mary), and whoever they have lined up for the industry night. After the class you are also put on their mailing list for possible future castings. Additionally, once you've completed their first class, you can sign up for special industry night workshops like reading copy in front of five commercial agents, or a cold reading class with a casting director. Yes, other places have similar industry nights for maybe less money, but Brooke's and Mary's usually have a really good line up because the industry in attendance knows they're going to see actors who have commercial training.

The class is currently $440 which isn't exactly cheap, but definitely worth it. For example, I met my commercial agent Phil Cassese in the class, and also booked three commercials from Brooke's and Mary's mailing list. Results may vary, but their class creates opportunities and gives you a foundation of skills to help take advantage of them when they knock.

Aside – Genealogy of Signing with an Agent

Just to clarify, Phil did not sign with me that night, or that week, or that year.

The week after our final Brooke and Mary class, I was preparing a follow-up mailing to send him when his assistant called me in for a meeting. He wanted to freelance with me. For a year he sent me out pretty regularly on auditions. I got several callbacks but didn't book a thing. So he stopped sending me out on auditions which is exactly what he should have done. I was on my own again, working the sites and techniques listed in other sections. Every time I booked something though, I'd briefly email Phil to let him know about it. He didn't always send a reply, but I didn't really expect one.

Then one day I booked a job I found on Actors Access with the *Onion News Network*. When I let him know about it, he wrote back, "Great, let me know when it comes out!" Progress! The video was supposed to be released within three months. I could wait that long; then it didn't come out for nine months. When I finally sent him the link he loved it and wrote back, "We have to get you out on some auditions!" He did, and later that spring I booked a role in a Castrol Motor Oil commercial as a grungy car mechanic. Sadly, due to the Gulf oil spill, it never aired. Plus, I was also getting more callbacks.

A few months later Phil hinted at having me come in sometime in the fall to sign with him. The fall came, and the big news was that Phil was switching agencies... I heard no more about signing. Maybe I should have brought it up to him myself, but I figured he was busy with the transition, and I am not good about that sort of thing anyway. So I went to one of Brooke's and Mary's industry nights to meet five new commercial agents just in case. They all wound up calling me about freelancing and started to send me out on auditions. Phil found out and said he thought he'd signed me and that we should make it official. (Signing has been compared to marriage. Now we have three kids and a house on Long Island.)

From first meeting to signing: four years. Your experience will vary.

SUMMARY

- Take Brooke's and Mary's class!

- If you don't live in New York, ask actors you know to recommend venues.

One-on-One – www.oneononenyc.com

One-on-One offers sessions and classes with industry that basically give you an opportunity to strut your stuff for them. What separates One-on-One from other such venues is that you have to pass a general audition before you can take their workshops. The idea is to ensure visiting industry that the people they are about to see will have at least a certain level of talent and are, therefore, less likely to be wasting their time. At the audition, you perform two monologues and, if you pass, you pay a onetime $50 fee. It may sound a bit scammy, but I know a surprising number of talented actors that did not pass their first audition.

For sessions, you either perform a monologue or sides (scene or commercial) for the agent, director, casting director, or manager of your choosing, and then talk with them a few minutes before it's time to move on with your life. These cost around $25-35 depending on how popular the session is. The first few of these I did, I performed a monologue and slowly realized that this was not my strong suit. From then on, I only signed up for sessions with agents that specifically wanted to see sides, or at least included it as an option.

Classes last anywhere from two hours to all day and are priced from around $80-300 depending on length and popularity. The industry person conducting the class, usually a casting director, will send you sides based on your headshot a day or two in advance. You'll perform your scene on-camera in class with a reader two or three times, receiving notes and adjustments from the CD. There is also usually a Q&A before or after the readings. After the class One-on-One emails you a link to your class footage that you can download and save for reference.

So are these sessions and classes worth it?

They can be as long as you are focused on what you are looking for and have done your research.

When you first sign-up with One-on-One, you can feel like a kid a candy store, and if you're not careful, find yourself out several hundred dollars before you know it. I signed up with the goal of finding a legit agent because a friend of mine had found his legit agent at One-on-One. So I wasted at least four sessions performing my monologue for legit agents before concentrating on sides that showcased my sense-of-humor (I actually got the sides from a One-on-One class with a CD from Fox).

By my count, I met eleven legit agents over the course of three months, and not one of them ever called me in. And, yes, I kept in touch with them when I had good news to share. Discouraging, no? Later I learned in an AFTRA seminar with Lisa Gold, the owner of Actors Connection, that, generally speaking, unless you're young and talented and beautiful, most agents don't want to take you from 0-60 but from 30-60. That means that they usually like to see that you can book work on your own before taking the time to work with you. Apparently my meager credits of the day weren't cutting it. Do I know this for a fact? No, but I have heard this put similar ways since.

How do I get legit credits without an agent?

Concentrate on taking the classes with casting directors who work on shows that utilize your type. *Vampire Diaries*, for example, does not seem to have many roles for someone of my type, so spending money on a class with the casting director for that show would probably be a waste of my resources. I took four classes at One-on-One with casting directors, and was later called in directly by two of them to audition for their respective shows, *30 Rock* and *Boardwalk Empire*. I booked neither role, but they at least liked my class performance enough to remember and consider me. This is also the kind of information you can share with agents to let them know that a casting director thinks enough of you to call you in.

This is also where research comes in. Before signing up for that class with the Casting Director of *Law & Order: SVU* call SAG-AFTRA and find out for how much longer the show will be shooting. If you take a class for a show that has only two weeks of shooting left, your opportunities will be fewer, and the CD might not remember you down the road when production starts back up again.

Most One-on-One new class alerts seem to come early in the morning, so don't sleep until noon if there is one you are on the look out for.

If a class is full and you are on the waitlist, check that class on the website after midnight. That's when the website is updated as to openings, but the email alerts for those openings aren't sent out until the next morning. This way you can hopefully get the jump on it.

And after you have a few "big" legit credits, start meeting with those legit agents.

Anything else I should know about One-on-One?

Yes, they also give you a space for a personal webpage where you can list credits, post headshots, and link to footage. About half a dozen people have contacted me for auditions after seeing me in the One-on-One files. Most of them were student productions (and mostly from Columbia University for some reason), but one was from casting director Stephanie Holbrook for an 'Untitled Elmore Leonard Project'. I did not book it, but it was still pretty cool. So fill out that web page and keep it up-to-date.

There is also a section of casting notices you can peruse. Most of them are student and unpaid, but keep checking.

Also, One-on-One rents out rooms in its facility to casting directors for auditions, so if you are in NYC you will hopefully have to visit it eventually.

But I live in LA.

There aren't as many as in New York, but One-on-One does have classes in LA. You can view the current list here: www.oneononenyc.com/la

SUMMARY

I have spent over $900 on One-on-One classes and sessions, and directly got two auditions as a result. Not so great. But they do tout many 'success stories' and hopefully I have passed some savings from personal lessons learned on to you:

- Have a plan!

- Unless you are young, talented, and beautiful, concentrate on classes with CDs for the shows right for your type. Get some credits and then meet some agents.

- Do your research. How much longer will this show be in production?

- Keep your One-on-One website up-to-date as industry does review them.

Actors Connection – www.actorsconnection.com

Actors Connection is similar to One-on-One in that they offer classes and seminars at comparable prices, but you don't have to audition to take them.

When you sign up, fill out the online profile so that industry will have some idea of what sides to send you when you register for their class. It is similar to your One-on-One webpage, but there is no place to link to your reels or footage. Also, no one has ever contacted me directly through Actors Connection about any roles, student or otherwise. Make of that what you will!

I have taken four classes from casting directors at Actors Connection and heard from none of them. But that happens, especially when I am slack about keeping in touch with them. I do have at least one friend who was brought in to audition for *30 Rock* after taking a class from one their casting directors. They also have posts of student 'success stories' so judge for yourself.

SUMMARY

Like One-on-One, your results with Actors Connection will vary. But again, do your research and decide what you are looking to do lest you risk the 'candy store' effect.

- Similar to One-on-One but no audition required

- Research, research, research before plunging in!

<u>Other Venues</u>

In New York, two other popular 'meet-and-greet' venues are The Actor's Green Room and The Network. I have attended class at neither, but heard enough positive things from friends to mention them here.

My LA actor friends largely recommend The Actor's Key.

FINAL THOUGHTS

There are many, many more venues in New York and LA, but the ones in this section I either have experience with, or have heard good things about. That doesn't mean other places are run by the Devil; it would simply be ridiculous to list every 'meet and greet' workshop here.

Have a plan and do your research before spending a lot of money. Ask actors you know and trust in your area for recommendations. We are social animals and asking which berries won't cause your skin to itch or your head to explode have helped keep us around for a while. Do the same with specific workshops and teachers so you get the most from your money.

Here is a disclaimer from the Actors Connection website that you can apply to the rest of them as well:

"Seminars or classes are for educational purposes only and will not secure or provide opportunity for employment in the field or representation by an agent."

OTHER WAYS TO FIND AUDITIONS

Mailings

You may have heard horror stories about assistants at agencies who are instructed to file actors' self-submitted headshots and resumes with cover letters directly into the garbage can. While I'm sure this has happened, it is not the gospel truth (see interviews below). A big part of an agent's job is to find new talent and how great to find them without having to leave his seat. That being said, I'm personally not a big fan of doing mailings. They are expensive and hard work. But who said this was easy?

First, do your research. *Call Sheet* formerly called *Ross Report*, contains the most up-to-date list of agents, casting directors, and managers in New York and Los Angeles. Look to see what kind of clients the agent represents and what kind of work (commercial, theater, print) they specialize in before mailing anything. Some even list an email to use for submissions. You can find *Call Sheet* at most major bookstores and specialty shops like the Tony award winning (seriously) 'Drama Book Shop' in New York City. It comes out currently twice a year in March and September and sells for $20. If you want to do a mailing, and the new *Call Sheet* comes out next week, you might want to wait for the new one in case that agent you were going to mail has switched agencies.

Several years ago I did a mailing to about 50 agents and managers in New York at a cost of about $100, and several hours of envelope addressing and stuffing work. I heard back from one agent… about extra work. Discouraging, yes? But I didn't have many strong credits on my resume and didn't have the greatest headshot at the time. If I were to do one now, I think (I *hope*) I would get more responses. Several of my friends have found their representation through mailings, so they do work. Or you might want to save your time and money for a workshop with multiple industry guests at Brooke and Mary.

Read *Acting As a Business* by Brian O'Neil

There are many books on what to do in the audition room, but this is one of the best ones I've read on how to get in the room into the first place.

One of the main things Brian points out is that many of the actors, big and small, you see on television and film were first noticed in the theater. After reading that, I began to notice that he was right. Not that you always have to have a background in theater to be a tv or movie star, but it can really help. He discusses this at length.

Brian also writes many other helpful things that I will leave for you to discover, copyright laws being what they are.

You can find his book at Amazon and probably in your local library system.

Check In with People Who Have Hired You Before

This may sound obvious, but it hadn't occurred to me until Lisa Gold said it in an AFTRA seminar. Someone who has shown the ultimate faith by hiring you once might be likely to do so again. They've worked with and, hopefully, still like you assuming you weren't a jerk or burned down the set. The day after I heard this, I emailed everyone I could think of that had previously hired me and said "Hello, how's it going?" Lo and behold, the producer wrote me back with an audition for a Nickelodeon promo he was working on. I didn't book the job, but it was nice to be called in and see him again. All because I'd taken the time to say "Hello."

Keep track of the people you've enjoyed working with and reach out when you've got some fun work to share or just to occasionally touch base and say, "Hi."

Follow-up with Industry Contacts
When You have Something to Follow-up About

This is similar to the previous section except it pertains to agents and casting directors that you have met in a class, but not necessarily been called in by yet. When you meet an agent or casting director in a seminar or class, find out how they prefer you get in touch with them.* Email/write them the next day saying how much you enjoyed the class and include links to good footage, and/or your website. Keep it short. After that, only contact them when you have some good news to share, like a booking or, better yet, a link to the finished product. Realize that if you don't get a response, it is probably because they are VERY busy. But after you've done enough work or, more importantly, enough work that they like, they may respond and even call you in for an audition or meeting. Don't inundate them because they get a LOT of emails, and even if they want to respond, it could be several days before they have a chance to do so. I would say be persistent but in this case, sometimes persistence can skirt the realm of annoyance. Let's just say "Don't give up." Industry wants to see and hear about the good work you've done.

*more on this in the interview section below

<u>Get Involved at an Improv Theater</u>

More and more casting directors are looking to improv theaters for talent (see interviews below). They attend their shows and search their web pages for performers. Also, as I mentioned earlier, they are great places to meet like-minded people to put on live shows and shoot videos. Plus, it is a lot of fun.

In New York, the big three improv theaters are the Magnet, UCB, and PIT. All of them have a page on their websites listing their performers, and casting directors do search these pages. Two of my friends were called in to audition for the short-lived television show *$#*! My Dad Says* by a casting director who found them on the Magnet performer page. A casting director I once auditioned for reconnected with me through the Magnet's web page about an audition for a show he was casting (unfortunately, I couldn't do it because it was non-union). There are many more examples. Plus, the theaters are sent breakdowns from people looking for improvisers for all kinds of projects and these get passed along, usually to their House team performers, but sometimes others as well.

Have you heard of Amy Poehler, Aziz Ansari, and Kristen Schaal? Guess where they all got their starts. Okay, some of that was stand-up, but they were all heavily involved with improv theaters as well.

In Chicago there is Second City, Improv Olympic(iO), and Annoyance Theatre. In LA, The Groundlings, UCB again, and iO West. In Atlanta there is Dad's Garage.

Different theaters in the same city can have different styles and vibes so shop around until you find the right one for you.

Plus, it is a lot of fun.

Tell Friends about Breakdowns You See That are Right for Them

This really helps *others* find auditions, but what are friends for?

If during your search you see a breakdown perfect for someone you know, forward it along. Not that you can read every breakdown with every actor you know in mind, but, occasionally I bet one will jump out at you.

I had an actor friend who passed away several years ago that strongly resembled Santa Claus. Whenever I saw a breakdown for someone resembling Saint Nick, I would always forward it to him. Sometimes he had already seen it, sometimes not, but he was always grateful. Help make someone's day while you still can.

You may hesitate to forward a casting that calls for someone 'old' or 'overweight' out of respect for your friend's feelings, but every 'senior' or 'plus-sized' breakdown I have forwarded to a friend has elicited a positive response. If your friend is an actor, they should embrace their type.

What if the breakdown is perfect for me *and* my friend?

Let your conscience be your guide. My first improv teacher told our class, "Remember, it's not show *friends*, it's show business." But then again, he was a dick.

'Like' Acting Organizations on Facebook

'Liking' the pages of theaters, casting directors, and publications on Facebook is a great way to stay informed and catch opportunities you might otherwise have missed. Theaters sometimes offer free shows. Casting directors occasionally post breakdowns they are having a difficult time casting. Workshop venues sometimes have specials on seminars and classes that haven't sold out. Backstage posts links to new articles and columns, and so on.

But I'm not on Facebook

Well, you really should be. As an actor, part of your job is networking. Your Facebook 'friends' are there to support you and for you to support them. And to share pictures.

Here is a partial list of acting related Facebook pages I 'Like' to give you some ideas of organizations to look for in your area and beyond:

Actors Connection NY – NYC seminars/workshops/classes (see previous section)
The Actor's Green Room – NYC seminars/workshops/classes (see previous section)
Backstage – so. many. great articles.
Bad Film Fest/Bad Theater Fest – friend's Festivals
Brooke Thomas Casting – See interview below!
Casting Loop – NYC actor updates, casting notices
Cherry Lane Theatre – NYC theatre
Ensemble Studio Theatre – NYC theatre company
Erica Palgon Casting and Beyond – see interview below
Flux Theatre Ensemble – NYC theatre group. Great people!
LAByrinth Theater Company - NYC theatre company
Liz Lewis Casting Partners – NYC casting house, occasionally posts breakdowns
Magnet Theater – best improv classes in NYC
Michael Howard Studios – where I studied acting (scene study, technique, etc.)
One-on-One NYC/LA – seminars/workshops/classes (see previous section)
Paladino Casting – NYC casting house
Play Submissions Helper – are you a playwright, or know one?
Primary Stages – Off-Broadway theatre company
The Queen's Secret Improv Club – Improv theater in Long Island City

Rattlestick Playwrights Theater – NYC organization for emerging playwrights

SAG-AFTRA – Oh, you know, that union

Second Stage Theatre Company – Off-Broadway theatre company

Stage 32 - Free social network for film, television, and theatre creatives

Steel City Improv Theater – founded by my friend Justin Zell, Pittsburgh, PA.

Survival Jobs for Actors – what it says

Youngblood - Ensemble Studio Theatre's company of playwrights under 30

There are a LOT more, but hopefully this will give you some ideas.

So get on Facebook, weather the puppy storm, and start connecting.

Intern at a Casting Office

A friend I met on a cable promo shoot got the gig because he had interned at the place that cast it. They called him in to audition, and he booked it. So if you have the time, it's something to consider. You'll also get a behind-the-scenes look at casting, and, who knows, maybe even find something you enjoy doing more than acting. It also helps if you're not a jerk.

Extra Work

Extras, I mean, *background artists*, are an essential part of most films and television shows. Yes, it can be long hours with little reward, but it is also a chance to be on a big set and see how things work behind the scenes. Sometimes, rarely, a background artist can get bumped up to a bigger role. Rarely. While I know it has happened other times, the only two instances I have heard of this happening was to an extra on *Deadwood* and my local bank teller who got her SAG card by sitting at a dinner table on a film with Nicole Kidman.

If you want to try extra work, you will see plenty of chances at 'Casting Networks' as discussed in the 'Internet' section. You can also contact these agencies in New York:

Central Casting – You've heard of them. They also have offices in LA.

Grant Wilfey Casting – They sometimes list what they are looking for on their website and have open registration days at the beginning of each month for union and non-union members. See their website for more information.

Sylvia Fay Casting – This one may not have as many projects as the other two, but they do send out their own notices. Registering on their website can take a while, so make sure you have several minutes if you choose to do so.

SAG Foundation LifeRaft videos

The Screen Actors Guild Foundation is an "educational, humanitarian and philanthropic" non-profit organization dedicated to helping actors, ostensibly those in SAG-AFTRA. Among the many helpful things they do is hold panels with industry professionals on a wide variety of topics relevant to actors like 'Excellence in Web TV: Creating, Marketing and Building an Audience for New Media' and then post videos of these panels on their webpage and YouTube. There are sixty-two videos posted as of this writing and they are currently available for anyone to view. Some recent topics include 'Hyphenate! - Becoming an Actor-Writer'; 'Form and Function: Creating a Unique and Agile Website'; 'Prepping for Pilot Season: Casting Directors'; 'Taped Auditions'; and 'Corner Your Market: Fostering Your Marketing Savvy'. I took notes on the 'Website' panel and forwarded them to my webmaster. There are also many 'conversation' or interview videos with actors like the casts and crews of *Lincoln* and *Silver Linings Playbook*.

Strictly speaking, you won't find auditions directly from these videos, but you will find much valuable information to help get you in the room, aid you once you're in there, and deal with the acting life in general.

<u>INTERVIEWS</u>

Some casting directors and agents and managers I know were nice enough to take the time from their SUPER busy schedules to answer some short questions via email. The longest one with my commercial agent Phil was done over lunch. You will see many different answers to the same questions and similar answers to the same questions. I learned a lot from these interviews and hope you do as well.

Casting Directors

Jason Buyer - www.jasonbuyer.com

BIO

The Casting Playhouse offers private one-on-one mock audition technique classes as well as group classes for all levels. The Casting Playhouse not only teaches audition technique, but self-confidence and control in uncomfortable yet realistic audition situations. Meet Jason Buyer, the CEO of The Casting Playhouse, now in NYC. Jason began casting extras and commercials in his home town of Chicago, Illinois, nearly twenty years ago. His casting background and experience is extensive. Jason was the senior casting coordinator at Warner Bros. TV, the casting associate at UDK Casting (Ulrich/Dawson/Kritzer), and the former casting associate at Weber and Associates Casting at MGM, working on and casting dozens of pilots and episodic television shows in Los Angeles. Jason continues to stay true to his roots, completing principal casting for the Columbia College and UCLA Directing & Writing Programs as well as the webseries, 'The Consultants,' and the pilot presentation, 'Odds On The Acts,' from creator Chris Bearde. Jason has also been the invited keynote speaker at numerous universities, Ohio State University, The University of Cincinnati, The University of Georgia, Clemson University, Columbia College, Chicago, Valparaiso University, The New School of Drama, Stonestreet Studios, etc. conducting marketing seminars for their graduating seniors and theatre students. Jason is also an adjunct professor for Columbia College, Chicago, running the Semester In LA Acting Program. He currently teaches adult classes at Anthony Meindl's Actor Workshop & Weist Barron Acting Studios in New York. Jason's book, *Inside The Audition Room: The Essential Actors Handbook For Los Angeles* is available at Samuel French Bookstores in LA, Amazon.com, and The Drama Bookshop in NY.

Were there any other ways aside from having representation that an actor could get in front of you?

Most of the time auditions would come from submitting or pitching an actor into our office. I would say ninety percent of the time an agent or a manager would submit or pitch an actor for a pre-read appointment. I did have my own workshop files when I was a guest, so cold reading workshops is another way to get in the door. When I first moved to LA, casting was not done online. There was a one day break between getting the breakdown completed and releasing it to the agents and managers. Now everything can be done online, and a breakdown can be done pretty quickly, at a moment's notice. In a pinch, I would go through my file of workshop actors and bring them in, if they fit the role.

Were there any other ways you'd meet new talent aside from representatives or cold reading workshops?

I would see a play or attend a showcase every once in a while. However, no one really cares too much about seeing theater on the West Coast. School showcases are great, but then there are the (non-school) showcases where an actor pays a flat rate to perform. School or class showcases are the way to go.

Referrals are huge. If I know your work, or if an actor friend of mine can vouch for you, there's a good chance we will take the risk and bring you in to audition, or even meet you for a general meeting, just to get to know you. Casting directors will usually find the time to pre-read an actor. If the actor is horrible it won't matter. You will just wasting my time, and it will be a long time before I bring you back. But if the actor is horrible in front of the producer or director, that makes me look bad. So anytime I would call someone in from a workshop, it was always be for a pre-read first even if I have seen your work previously. Even if you blew me away at a workshop, I'd still bring you in to read for me first. You can be a great workshop actor, but mixed in with a bunch of other actors who have series regulars and guest star credits on their resume – you might not be as good as I had originally thought. I won't take the chance. It doesn't hurt me to pre-read you first.

What do actors who get a lot of callbacks have in common?

Most of the actors who get called back did a really good job of owning the room while making specific choices with the material. I talk a lot about not giving away your power. Every actor has a lot of power walking into the room, so even though we are auditioning you, try and turn the tables a bit and make it feel as if you are auditioning us. Take control of your power: make sure you're not apologizing all the time. Make sure you're not asking us to do it a second time. Make sure you're not judging your work as you are working. These are all things that we see from the casting side. It's quite obvious when you have given up your power. We don't think, "I'm going to give this person six thousand dollars for a guest spot for a week because he seems nice." The character probably isn't fearful – the actor may be. A lot of it may come down to allowing yourself to feel comfortable in an uncomfortable situation or setting. It's certainly not easy to do. You don't always have to be the best actor to book the job, but it certainly helps. Sometimes it can just be about type. Although he may not be the strongest actor we have seen that day, the director might choose him because he fits the part physically.

What do actors who get a lot of bookings have in common?

Besides the fact that they all have excellent representation (agent and manager), they come in with strong choices. You don't necessarily have to give a repeat performance of your original read. Try to keep it fresh without giving me something new. Use what you brought in to the original reading. You did get called back after all. We probably don't want to see a carbon copy of what you just did because it's going to feel stale.   Keep it honest and engaging. Own your choices and just surrender. In the producer's session, it's pretty clear who books the job and who doesn't. It might come down to one or two top choices, but it becomes pretty clear to the people in the room - the director, writer, producer —who's going to get the job.

Why is it harder to find legit auditions than commercial ones?

When casting commercials, we are looking for real people. It doesn't necessarily matter if you are a union or non-union actor for a commercial because a commercial CD can and will Taft-Hartley[1] an actor and get him into the union. Commercially, we will most likely see you even if you aren't in the union. For film and television, we bring in roughly ten to twelve people for the producers to see. Six to eight people for a co-star. A casting director might pre-read ten, twenty, fifty people if he has time to do so, all based on your representation and the union status of the project. If you are a non-union actor who is submitted for a union project, you may not get the opportunity to audition. If you a non-union actor who gets the rare opportunity to read for a union project and you end up being the choice that for that role, it's possible we will end up going to our second choice because you are non-union. Again commercially, we don't really care. The other problem is that more and more feature film actors are doing television which makes it more difficult for everyone (except for the actor who has the offer). You will have to be with one of the better agencies to even get the opportunity to audition for a major feature film. Audition information for major feature films may not even be released through the breakdowns. Casting directors will just call the top talent agencies and managers and ask who they have that fits the breakdown.

Sounds discouraging.

It is. Just know that your representation does matter, especially in the world of film and television. In Los Angeles, you can have only one theatrical agent, one commercial agent, one print agent, one voice over agent, etc. They can all be from the same agency, but only one of each. In New York and Chicago, you can freelance with many different agencies.

So even if you have several tv credits, unless you have better representation, it's harder to get in the room?

Credits certainly help. Having a great reel will help. But it will always be harder getting in the room without good representation, either by an agent, a manager, or both.

**Is there one direction or note you find yourself giving a lot to beginning
actors or actors in general?**

It depends if you are asking me as an acting coach or casting director. When I cast, I don't bother to look and see who represents you. I'll read you regardless of who you're with as long as you physically look the part. I know that I will be able to work with you and give you exact notes, based on what I need. I always know what makes up a good audition and what seems lacking, and I can easily express what I need. I feel like there are so many actors that are so focused on what they have to do that they stop listening and being in the present. I think the best advice I can give any actor is to make sure that the story is the most important thing. Let go of what you have to do as an actor, and allow yourself to be in it – be in the now. If you make the story the most important thing, you won't worry about remembering your lines or if you messed up. Listen and stop judging your work as you are working. Stay in the scene and enjoy your new reality. You don't need to make it so difficult.

Can you give a specific example of actors putting the story before themselves?

Actors get in their heads all the time, always thinking about what they have to do. So much so that they stop listening. If you can just allow yourself to be in the situation that you are in and *not* worry so much about memorizing your lines or cue words that trigger your response, then you will be in much better shape in the audition room. Try to let go of control and live in the unknown. As an audience, we want to feel connected to something. It's really about staying true to what is happening now. A casting director is an audience first. If you're so focused on what you have to do as an actor - whether you're going to get the job, or how you are going to pay your rent... all of that acting bullsh-t that comes from inside your head (This isn't what the character is thinking, after all), then your audition isn't going to go very well.

Is there one thing you wish you could magically stop all actors from doing in auditions, or have them do?

Anytime you leave the audition room and then come back and ask do it again, I think that's a huge "no". I've probably read 10,000 actors to date, and I've never had an actor come back into the audition room, read again and actually book the job. It's never happened.

You mean they literally left the room and asked to come back in?

Yes.

How many people do that?

I've probably seen a dozen or so. Not a lot but it happens. Most of the time the actor is asking to come back in because in his brain he is thinking that he could have done a better job. It's just one of those acting things that almost every actor does. You've just got to let it go! Love your work and be okay with the choices you have made. Don't always think that it will be better the second time around. Most people don't get a second chance. Be great the first time.

Another pet peeve of mine is when an actor erases the punctuation on the paper. It drives me crazy! Some actors tell me that their old acting teacher told them not pay attention to the punctuation on the paper. It's not about you and what you want to do. It's about the story and moving the story forward. If you take out the punctuation in a half-hour sitcom audition, you probably will kill every single joke. The script is the blue print for what the writers are looking for. We want you to be free and creative within the confines of the story. Drives me nuts – and makes no sense.

An actor once told me in a seminar she was teaching that actors should put a button on the end of a script. Like a last little tagline, I guess to be more memorable. Is that a 'no, no' or is that good advice for legit?

I think it's a great piece of advice for commercials. I don't think it will work when you are auditioning for film and television. I don't think it will hurt you though. If you are putting a tag line at the end of a television or film audition, you're basically done. It may even lighten the mood. Commercially I know it works, not sure about using it with your theatrical auditions, however.

Any other advice to new actors or to actors in general?

It's a business. I would recommend every actor volunteer at a casting office once a week to learn about how the business works. Everyone needs free help these days. A lot of actors feel like if they go to school, they take a class, and they have a headshot, they are ready. A lot of actors are also hesitant on seeking outside advice because all you need is one job to call yourself an actor — even if it's extra work. I feel like the more knowledgeable you are about the business, the smarter career decisions you will make moving forward. I learned a ton just as a casting assistant from sitting in the audition room and taping all of the auditions. It was great seeing all of these huge celebrities coming in and auditioning. Your business needs to be an equal combination of marketing and talent.

What is the craziest thing you've seen someone do in an audition?

Well, this wasn't in an actual audition, but there was somebody who came into our casting office who dropped off a pizza with a headshot attached inside the box. The actor hand delivered it and said, "I'd love to be called in. Is there anything I can do? Can I do your laundry?" I've been fortunate, and although I've seen actors make hundreds of mistakes inside the room, I'm lucky that I haven't seen anything crazy. I would just remind actors not to come across as desperate. I did a cold reading workshop in Los Angeles several years ago and read this actress who I thought was pretty good, but who didn't blow me away. I had no plans of keeping her headshot or bringing her in to audition in a pinch. I just wasn't blown away that day. That was Octavia Spencer. Oops. You just never know. She won an Academy Award for *The Help*. She's doing really well for herself — clearly she didn't need me to bring her in. A long time ago, we cast a show called 'Soldier of Fortune' and brought in a bunch of people to read for the role of the clerk. There must have been five or six lines, and one of the girls I brought in was Selma Blair. She wasn't a big star at the time, but as soon as she was done with her audition, I knew she was going to book it — which she did. She was very confident in the room and made great choices for a role that had a couple of lines.

Anything else, maybe about representation....?

At the end of the day, it won't matter who is representing you as long as they are doing their job and getting you out. Are you getting the opportunities to succeed? There are some big actors who are with smaller agencies. When I was starting out in casting, one of the guys we used to bring in all the time was Bryan Cranston. He was with the House of Representatives for a very long time. He always did great work and was always respectful. He's now with United Talent Agency – but at the time he had a great relationship with a smaller agency, and his agent got him out all the time. It's just so important to have someone who really believes in you. This could be an agent or a manager. Maybe both. You just need the opportunity to showcase what you can do.

*from the SAG-AFTRA website: "The Taft-Hartley Act is a US Federal labor law enacted by Congress in 1947. As it relates herein, the law allows a signatory producer to hire a non-union performer if that non-union performer possesses a quality or skill essential to the role and an available union performer with the needed quality or skill cannot be found. When hiring a non-union performer for a SAG-AFTRA covered role, you must submit to the union a Taft-Hartley report with the performer's information, the reason for hire and the performer's headshot."

Stacy Gallo - www.stacygallocasting.com

BIO

Stacy Gallo has been a casting director in New York City for the past 10 years. She began her career at MTV as a casting assistant and was then promoted to casting director on a live show. In 2001, she was chosen to create an in-house casting company for Hungry Man, called Downstairs Casting and headed that department for 7 years. In 2008, she ventured out on her own and formed her own company, Stacy Gallo Casting. To her credit, she has been successful in casting a variety of projects, including many national network commercials for notable directors and clients.

With a background in acting herself, Stacy completed the 2-year program at the William Esper Studio in New York. She has a reputation for being a very actor-friendly casting director. She really knows how to make actors feel comfortable in an audition and is adept at bringing out their comedic side by showing them how to enhance their performance for the commercial.

In addition to her busy casting schedule, Stacy also teaches a commercial improv class at The Upright Citizen's Brigade. Because of her expertise in the field of casting, many of her students have secured positions with top commercial agents and have booked national commercials. Stacy also teaches a popular On-Camera Commercial Class at One-on-One NYC which has assisted actors in getting parts in high profile commercials.

Some of her most memorable and award-winning spots include NY Lottery Little Bit of Luck, CareerBuilder.com Superbowl Campaign, Tribeca Film Festival, McDonalds, CNN campaign, Luvs, AT&T, Yoplait, ESPN, Mastercard w/Brett Favre, Verizon Wireless, and Visa w/ Kevin Bacon.

In your bio it says many students from your class go on to work with commercial agents. How does that happen?

In the 3rd week of my class at One-on-One, an agent comes for a showcase. More often than not, at least one actor gets called in by that agent. There have been times (in both my UCB class and at One-on-One) that an agent has not called in an actor that I think is amazing, so I will recommend that actor to another agent.

My hope is that actors are better prepared after my class to audition for agents.

Aside from your classes and agents, are there any other ways you find and meet new talent?

Yes! I have met people on the street, train, supermarket etc. I approached Grizz from *30 Rock* at a restaurant by my house years ago before the show and ended up casting him in a Mastercard commercial with Brett Favre.

I use Casting Networks and Actors Access all of the time and find new talent that way. Sometimes I am looking for a specific look or talent, but also just to find new faces. I also meet people through referrals from other actors or people that I know.

I also look on the UCB, PIT and Magnet performer pages.

If I can get out to a show, I often find new talent that way too.

Sometimes the same breakdown is posted on multiple websites like Actors Access AND Casting Networks, for example. In your experience, is that because it's difficult to cast certain roles and the casting director is widening her net, or is it a time issue? Do you think talent should submit to every posting of that breakdown they find or just the first one?

I definitely post on multiple websites if I am casting for a very specific role and also just to see as many new faces as possible. (Some of my directors only want to see fresh faces on every job which can be challenging!)

It can be a time issue as well, but, usually, it is just to get the word out using more than one resource.

I would rather an actor just post on one website, otherwise it gets confusing, and we may give the same actor 2 slots in the schedule.

Is there one direction or note you find yourself giving a lot to beginning actors or even actors in general?

Stop acting. Just be yourself in commercials. We want you to feel real and not like you are selling us something. Don't put-on. And, don't be afraid, when asked, to make the copy your own and to have fun with it.

Improv skills seem to be hot right now and possibly will be until the end of on-camera media as we know it. When is it okay to improvise in an audition? If the copy notes don't specifically state to improvise or stick straight to the script, should the actor ask first or just go ahead and improvise and see if you reign them in? Which is less awkward?

I think an actor should always ask if it is ok to improvise if the casting director or camera operator does not say anything either way. Many times we will say things like, "Don't be afraid to make it your own" or " Have fun with the copy" or "You don't have to stick to the copy verbatim." This all means it is ok and usually encouraged to improvise. I work with directors who feel very strongly about sticking to the copy (many of these directors were copywriters at one point.) But in many cases directors want to see what an actor can bring to the copy by making it his own and not being afraid to improvise. I encourage all actors pursuing a commercial career to take an improv class because it is such an important skill in auditioning for commercials.

What do actors who get a lot of callbacks have in common?

CONFIDENCE! Not being afraid to be themselves. Not putting on –
just
playing it very real – and also not bring afraid to improvise when asked to do so. It makes them memorable if they take a chance and make us laugh with one of their own ideas. I always tell actors, we usually see 75+ actors per role, so you may as well take a chance and try and stand out.

After you've met an actor in a class or elsewhere, how do you prefer that they follow-up with you, and when or under what circumstances do you think it's appropriate for an actor to do so?

Email. I never mind when an actor (that I know or have met) invites me to a show, lets me know if they are working with a new agent, sends an updated headshot, or follows up with me after class.

Brette Goldstein – www.brettegoldstein.com

BIO

Brette Goldstein has been casting films and commercials in NYC for over 12 years.

Films Brette has cast have gone on to win a multitude of awards and been official selections at Cannes, Sundance, Tribeca, Hamptons, Woodstock, SxSW, LA FF, Woods Hole, Clermont-Ferrand, DC Shorts, NY International, Philadelphia, Boston, Austin, Bahamas International, Great Lakes, Sante Fe and the IFP Film Market to name just a few.

In addition, Brette has cast commercials, promos and industrials for Nickelodeon, MasterCard, Coca-Cola, and Papa Johns among others.

She was the resident casting director at the **Folger Elizabethan Theatre** for nine seasons. She also handled the casting for Source Theatre Company, Washington Shakespeare Company and Washington Jewish Theatre.

Brette also worked on the casting for several LORT theatres while working at Elissa Myers Casting, Michelle Ortlip Casting and Charles Rosen Casting.

She coaches privately and teaches acting and audition technique workshops and classes at studios and universities.

Why do you cast both commercials and legit projects? Is that unusual? What are the advantages and disadvantages?

I like casting both commercial and legit projects. Keeps me on my toes. There's such a different pace and energy to both mediums...they are so different. I've recently thrown television into the mix, and that has its own thing going on. I like and value variety and a new adventure with every project.

Aside from classes and representation, are there any other ways you find and meet new talent?

Shows, showcases, workshops, friends of friends and relatives, professional referrals, college seminars...I meet new talent all the time and everywhere. When I was coming up as a young casting director in

Washington, DC, we were not a town of reps and names, so a good casting director was recognized for bringing new talent into the mix. It was a tight community, so discovering fresh, hot talent was highly regarded. I still strive to make all of my schedules consist of at least half unrepresented actors. It makes me feel like I'm doing my job right!

What do actors who get a lot of callbacks have in common?

They're well-prepared, they take a moment before they begin the scene, they stay connected with their reader and out of their heads, they listen to and take adjustments and when they leave the studio they leave…they go back to their full, rich lives, as opposed to stressing out over what we think of them. These wonderful actors bring their own unique energy, voice, humor and way of processing life's hurdles to the character. They're not thinking about what we want them to be. If one thinks about it, it's a lot like dating, isn't it?

What do actors who get a lot of bookings have in common?

Same as above.

When is it okay to improvise in an audition? If the copy notes don't specifically state to improvise or stick straight to the script, should the actor ask first or just go ahead and improvise and see if you reign them in? Which is less awkward?

Good question. I think actors should improv a little with comedic material. Improv is so important nowadays. Just be good at it. I have to admit, it's painful to watch comedic material with improv thrown in that was better, well, left scripted. Improv is a muscle. Ya gotta keep working it. It's fine to ask up front, but most actors nowadays just put their own spin on the sides or copy. We can always see a take without.

Is there one direction or note you find yourself giving a lot to beginning actors or actors in general?

I will often ask, "What do you want?", "What is the relationship here?", "Where are you in space and time?" Often actors have to think about the answers for a bit. They shouldn't need to do that. Those questions are the first questions they should have asked themselves in their preparation. I will often ask beginning actors to not feel that they have to fill the room with their voice. Your voice should only extend to your reader. Theatre actors who are transitioning into film and television will often work from the outside in, with big performances to boot. It's important for actors to watch themselves on tape. Watching their own footage can often provide the greatest lessons. I also find myself saying, especially to women, "Would you have handled the situation that way?" Usually I'll ask this if they leap into a full-scale argument in the scene. People don't do that in life so much. The real dramatic tension is in the subtleties. The passive aggression. The manipulation. The not wanting to alienate themselves or the other person but still get their way. That's just my taste, though.

Is there one thing you wish you could magically stop all actors from doing in auditions, or have them do?

I'd have them well-prepared enough, on all levels, to nail it on the first take. I don't mind working with actors in the room (I love it, in fact); however, especially with commercial casting (when I've added several more actors per hour to a schedule), actors often feel like the moment they enter the room we have more than enough time and patience to see as many takes as they need to get it right. Actors from the five most prestigious commercial agencies in New York will often come in and not only need ten takes to get one that works, they expect ten takes. That doesn't seem fair to me and my team, especially since it's those very people that are schmoozing with their friends and colleagues in the lobby, as opposed to taking a look at their copy. My relationships, both personally and professionally, are built on trust. I value actors' time and I expect that same in return.

Do you have any advice in terms of getting auditions for actors just starting out who don't have an agent?

Heck, I am all for getting the breakdowns illegally if you can! Sometimes it's the only way to really see what's out there. In the meantime, Actors Access, NYCastings, Backstage, Casting Frontier, Casting Networks, Mandy, etc.

Any other advice to new actors or actors in general?

Be a pro. Be on time. Be prepared. Be honest. Be fun. Be nice. Be true to yourself.

What is the craziest thing you've seen someone do in an audition?

A middle aged man was reading a scene where the character was on the phone and continued his conversation while pooping on the toilet. This guy clearly takes his clothes off to poop. So, he strips down to his boxer shorts while continuing to read the scrip/talk on his cell phone. He slides down the back wall, close to the floor, to simulate sitting on a toilet. (Yes, there were chairs in the room.) His boxers, which may have been as old as I was at the time, were quite flimsy and scooted to the side as he talked and poop-grunted while holding his audition sides. He didn't notice that his balls were just barely grazing the floor. Good times!

Angela Mickey – www.lizlewis.com

BIO

Angela Mickey is the Managing Director of Casting for Liz Lewis Casting Partners and has worked there for over thirteen years, casting on-camera commercials, voice over, TV, film, and theater. Some recent commercial projects include Philadelphia Cream Cheese, Time Warner Cable, Cialis, Verizon Wireless, Exxon Mobil, AT&T, Revlon, Canadian Club, and more. Recent film projects include *Happy & Bleeding, 23 Blast, Wifed Out*, as well as ongoing projects *Dear Jen, Ante Up, Wrinkles*, and *Uncanny Valley*. TV projects include *Hunted by the Mob, Lazytown* for *Kids Sprout, My Life is a Lifetime Movie* and the animated series *Peter Rabbit*.

Aside from classes and agents, are there any other ways you find and meet new talent?

As a Casting Director, I feel like I am always on the lookout for talent. Even though I may speak to agents, I still have to be familiar with the talent out there. I attend showcases, plays, stand-up, sketch comedy, improv, music venues...anywhere I can find someone with talent. I search out reels and websites that feature videos from performers. I am also known to sometimes be out casually with friends and see someone I think is interesting and hand them a card so that I can bring them in for something. In this day and age, you never know what type of person you will be asked to find, and so many people are talented in multiple areas. You never know where the gem might be.

Is there one direction or note you find yourself giving a lot to beginning actors or even actors in general?

The one note is to be true to yourself - make choices, and don't be afraid to be wrong. Your first read may not be the best, but if I can see you made a choice, then I know that I can direct you differently. And honestly, if all actors did it perfectly without direction, then I'd be out of a job! It's normal that I would have to adjust you to bring you in line with production's view. It's why I have in-depth conversations before the casting even begins.

Do you have any advice in terms of getting auditions for actors just starting out who don't have an agent?

Network, network, network. If you don't have an agent, then it is your responsibility to get to know casting directors. The best way to do that is to get up in front of them. I know, as actors, you have to pick and choose where you spend money. But spending it to take a class from a casting director, or do one of the one-on-one meet and greets is a much more effective way to spend your money. Keep in mind, as a casting director, I'm not looking for "types" to fill my stable of actors - that's an agent's job. I'm looking for actors I can DIRECT. And you are also never done learning; there's no school for casting (yet) and all casting directors have different approaches to getting performances out of actors (even casting directors within the same office). So there is always something new to learn.

When is it okay to improvise in an audition? If the copy notes don't specifically state to improvise or stick straight to the script, should the actor ask first or just go ahead and improvise and see if you reign them in? Which is less awkward?

I think there is always some room to make scripts conversational, and you really have freer reign with comedic projects. When things are more serious, or if it is a medical commercial and there are legal parameters, well, no one wants to make up a side effect or forget one! You will begin to recognize which casting directors tend to encourage freer reads, and for those that you are unsure about, well, ask! It's your audition, your attempt to get a job. For those 5 or 10 minutes it's YOUR studio, and don't be afraid to get the information you need so you can audition effectively. But if you do improv, don't be surprised or take offense if the Casting Director does one take as written; we usually are just making sure we are covering our bases.

Are there any current trends in casting that you've noticed?

It's pretty consistent to what you've seen over the years: lots of comedy commercials, lots of testimonial speaking-straight-to-camera spots, lots of life projects. If anything, with the slacking economy, we are seeing a lot of return to goods that families buy: household cleaning items, food items, and less about non-necessity goods and restaurants.

What do actors who get a lot of callbacks have in common?

They make choices. They aren't afraid to embrace themselves with all of their little idiosyncrasies. And they don't fall into the trap of doing what they think is right or what they think we want. They read through it, make a few choices, and then come in the room and just let it go without over thinking it.

What do actors who get a lot of bookings have in common?

Some of this you can't pinpoint because there are a lot of aspects that come into play: demographics, how the group of actors play off of each other, how they represent all that the producers are hoping to show the audience. But the big thing is people who don't shoot themselves in the foot during the callback. It's important to read the room when you walk in. Do people seem tense? Then don't go around getting into their space or shaking their hands. Do people seem friendly? Then say "hi" when they greet you. Make sure to do what the director asks you to do and really listen. I see a lot of actors talk over the director when they are being given direction, and so they miss things. Or they act resistant, saying things like "oh, so we are going in a different direction than the original audition?" Yes! That's why it's a callback! Sometimes the director wants to try to perfect a performance but sometimes they just want to find out if you will do what they ask you to.

What is the "craziest" thing you've seen someone do in an audition?

I brought in Aubrey Plaza for a Comedy Central audition. The scene was three disaffected data entry employees sitting in the break room bored out of their minds. Aubrey started tearing off pieces of paper and eating it. Her scene partners didn't know what to do, so they just reacted like it was normal. Hysterical. I wish I'd kept the footage.

Erica Palgon - www.ericapalgon.com

BIO

After almost 20 years in the business, Erica's experience has run the casting gamut for every specification you can think of: comedy, drama, subtle, over-the-top, real people, dry, wry, voice-over, spokesperson, unique special skills, languages, every shape, size, age, ethnicity, union and non-union.

She's worked on big projects, small projects and everything in between – casting indie films, award-winning documentaries, blockbuster studio pictures, and national spots for the Superbowl.

Aside from classes and agents, are there any other ways you find new talent?

When I am looking for new talent, I try to focus my searches on the areas that are the toughest to cast. Like most casting directors I attend theater, film, watch a lot of tv and, of course, go through all the invites and headshots/resumes that I get in the mail and email. It's hard to go to everything, so when I can't go, someone from my office will attend. I have found quite a lot of really great actors at the acting schools where I have been a guest. I also love going to sketch comedy and meeting comedy people, so I go where those people are (comedy clubs and sketch shows in and around NYC). Along with some of the more mainstream types of shows/films, I also like slightly off beat and unique shows that may fall under the radar.

Do you have any advice regarding getting auditions for actors just starting out who don't have an agent?

Once you have solid training, the two key things to make sure you have are an acting resume and a professional headshot that looks like you. How you market yourself is very important. Make sure the resume is formatted correctly and easy to read and your headshot is a clear representation of you. The next thing you want to do is put your picture and resume on the websites that are most used by casting directors. Actors Access and Casting Networks are the two websites where casting directors post projects they are working on. Be smart about which roles you submit yourself for. Don't submit just to get the attention of the casting director when you are clearly not right for the role. It leaves a bad impression. Two other good resources are Backstage and Theatrical Index.

It's also important to create strong working relationships in the industry. A good way to start is by making connections with up and coming filmmakers. Student filmmakers are always looking for talent for their projects, and most of them don't know where to find actors. These are the filmmakers of tomorrow and where you should build these relationships. Make a good impression and they will remember you as their careers climb. It's a great way to get used to auditioning. And if you do book a role in a student film, you could have the beginnings of an acting reel that could help lead to future auditions.

Remember that projects start with writers, producers, and directors. Casting directors, agents, and managers all come aboard much later in the process. Network with all members that make up this industry and be seen. Try to go to events where you can learn something about the industry, not just where you are expecting to get work. Go to industry events where you are 1 of 3 actors rather than 1 of 1000. Be genuine and honest when talking to people. Don't sell yourself. The decision makers respond to strong, real personalities.

Remember this isn't an overnight process. Put in the work, be creative and give it time.

Is there one direction or note you find yourself giving a lot to beginning actors or even actors in general?

I'd say the biggest misconception is that the acting business is easy. That you can "get into this" by saying I want to be an actor, take one class and boom! Acting is like any other profession. It requires a commitment to training and professionalism. Many people lose out on work because of how unprofessional they present themselves and how little work they put into their training.

Take your acting training seriously and you will benefit greatly from the results. All professions require proper training and acting is no different. On the professional point, most actors, beginners or not, disregard professionalism in acting, because it's 'art', a 'craft', but they forget it is a business. I am frequently asked to speak on industry panels, and it is very disappointing to hear that the common problem we all have with actors is their lack of professionalism. It's really one of the few things actors can control and the one thing that most pay the least attention to. The thing to remember is this is a trust business and it's collaborative. We all work very hard to pull projects together and if one person doesn't do his job, we all are affected in one way or another. Think of yourself in one giant office. Not working alone. You need to not only present yourself well but also those who are putting their faith in you from casting directors, agents, managers to producers, directors and everyone in between. Present your best self to people and you will, in turn, get the best results.

When do you think it is okay to improvise in an audition?

Every audition is different. The best way to know when to improv is to ask the person auditioning you. Always ask first!

Aside from the material, what are some differences between commercial and legit auditions?

In commercials most spots are between 30-60 seconds long. A lot needs to be conveyed in that short amount of time. You also are given a very short amount of time to prepare for commercial auditions, at most 10 minutes, prior to going into the audition room.

For legit auditions there really isn't a time limitation. You are given a few pages (sides) to prepare a few days ahead of time. Casting directors schedule actors for a specific time to come to audition.

Overall, auditions for commercials and film are becoming more similar in feel, as a lot of filmmakers these days work on commercials and vice versa.

What do actors who get a lot of callbacks have in common?

They make strong choices, are confident in what they are doing, and can take direction very well.

What do actors who get a lot of bookings have in common?

They make strong choices, are confident in what they are doing, and can take direction very well.

After you've met an actor in a class or elsewhere, how do you prefer they follow-up with you, and when or under what circumstances do you think it's appropriate for an actor to do so?

When they have something to say. Not just, 'hey I'm here, hire me.' Are you in a show, film, tv show? Did you book something recently, get a callback? Something worth talking about.

Is there one thing you wish you could magically stop all actors from doing in auditions?

Don't be afraid! Casting directors and directors want to see strong choices. We are open to YOUR take on roles. Stop second guessing your instincts. Be bold, wise and confident in your auditions and you will have success.

Lisa Rubenstein - www.rubensteincasting.com

BIO

Lisa Rubenstein is the owner and casting director of NYC based Rubenstein Casting. She casts for commercials, voiceovers, print, film and television.

Some On-camera commercial credits include Pepsi, Verizon Droid, Dunkin' Donuts, Xbox, Newcastle Brown Ale, and New Jersey Lottery.

Some of her Voiceover casting credits include Cheerios, Miller Genuine Draft, Hilton Hotels, Crest Toothpaste, Citibank, and Big Brothers Big Sisters.

Lisa's improv/comedy background and agent relationships have led to a variety of projects for television and the web, including the television pilot *The Reclaimers* starring John Lutz and Seth Kirschner.

She also recently cast the feature *A Friend Will Help You Move*. Recent short films include *What Cheer* with Richard Kind, *Space Cadet* with Jessica Hecht, and *Kid Deville* with Adam Shapiro.

Rubenstein Casting has a mission to give back. For each project Lisa casts, a percentage of the casting profits goes to an organization of the client's choice.

What inspired you to donate a portion of your casting proceeds to charity?

I have always felt that I am so lucky to be in this business and have my dream career. So when I opened my company, I wanted to do something that would help others. For each project cast, a percentage of my profits go to an organization of that client's choice. Some clients always want to donate to the same charity if they feel strongly about one. Others like to switch it up.

Aside from classes and agents, are there any other ways you find and meet new talent?

I also find talent going to theatre, comedy shows and at college showcases. I have also found talent when someone refers me to a new actor's website.

Do you have any advice for actors just starting out who don't have an agent in terms of getting auditions?

Network, Network, Network. And create work. Don't just wait for opportunities to come to you, create your own opportunities. For example, get together with your actor friends, create a comedy group, and make a few videos. Make a website and put your work out there.

Is there one direction or note you find yourself giving a lot to beginning actors or even actors in general?

Understand your character's story in the script and the story as a whole. This works for commercial auditions and legit auditions. You never know what will happen when you go in the audition room so you need to be prepared for anything. Knowing the lines is great but knowing the story and what is happening is even more important. This way, if you lose your place or forget a few words, you can put it in your own words and stay in character because you know what you are talking about. Also, sometimes the director or casting director will talk to you about the script or ask you to read another scene that maybe you didn't practice.

When is it okay to improvise in an audition? If the copy notes don't specifically state to improvise or stick straight to the script, should the actor ask first, or just go ahead and improvise and see if you reign them in? Which is less awkward?

Usually it is good to improvise. Many clients actually want the actors to improvise. It is a really important part of being an actor. Especially in comedy. If you are not sure, then ask. Can't hurt to ask. If you are coming in to audition for me, I am happy to answer any questions. Part of my job is to make sure you understand the character and you give the best audition possible. I want you to be amazing. So ask away.

What do actors who get a lot of callbacks have in common?

They are really good, natural actors. They are believable in the role and they can take direction. Each take isn't the same.

After you've met an actor in a class or elsewhere, how do you prefer that they follow-up with you?

Email is always best.

Brooke Thomas – www.brookethomascasting.com

BIO

Brooke Thomas has been a commercial casting director in New York City for over 17 years. She has worked at Liz Lewis Casting and most recently at House Casting before starting her own venture Brooke Thomas Casting. Brooke has cast over 2000 commercials for brands such as ETrade, NY Lottery, Red Lobster, Pizza Hut, Charles Schwab and Huggies. She has cast for directors such as Robert Altman, Fredrik Bond, Dave Meyers, Clay Williams, Stan Schofield, Mark Tiedemann, and many others.

In addition to being a full-time casting director, Brooke also teaches with Mary Egan, a word-of-mouth, always-sold-out, award-winning commercial class for aspiring actors(see previous section).

Brooke began her professional life as an actress and performer. She worked in regional theater, summer stock and with the renowned improv comedy troupe ImprovBoston. Her actor training has proved to be an invaluable asset in her career as a casting director.

Brooke lives in Tribeca with her two teenage children, a high school sweetheart, and an opinionated Shih Tzu.

Why did you and Mary decide to start your commercial class in the first place?

Mary and I had both been teaching commercial classes at other facilities. We both agreed that the classes weren't personal enough. Half the battle of successful auditioning is being comfortable and confident in the room. We felt that a smaller class size would allow for a more personal experience and allow the actor to feel free and comfortable on camera.

While I know it's dependent on talent and marketability and largely out of your hands, do you know approximately what percentage of your students get called by industry after your classes? What advice would you give to people who don't initially get a call?

I would say that 75% of our students get calls after our class either to audition for projects we are working on or from agents met at the class or solicited after our class. The calls may or may not be immediately following the class. They may be months later. You have to keep at it. Keep in contact with agents and casting directors to let them know what you are working on, what auditions/callbacks you have gotten, and when they can come and see you perform. Actors should continue pursuing auditions and work on their own all the time, even if they have agents.

Aside from your class and agents, are there any other ways you find and meet new talent?

Attending shows is a great way to meet new talent. I was working on a film for a director friend of mine. He was having a difficult time finding the lead guy. I attended a reading that a friend produced and, lo and behold, the lead in the reading was perfect for the film. I put the director in contact with the actor and boom! Match made.

Is there one direction or note you find yourself giving a lot to beginning actors or even actors in general?

Keep it real. Stop acting. Actors want to act; I get it. But in the commercial world it's all about you just being yourself on camera. Don't push; try and relax.

When is it okay to improvise in an audition? If the copy notes don't specifically state to improvise or stick straight to the script, should the actor ask first, or just go ahead and improvise and see if you reign them in?

Mary and I believe that it is always okay to improvise within reason in an audition. Clearly you must not re-write the copy, but allowing yourself to improvise gives you freedom for *you* to come through.

What do actors who get a lot of callbacks have in common?

Confidence.

What do actors who get a lot of bookings have in common?

Confidence, patience, good biz skills.

What is the craziest thing you've seen someone do in an audition?

There was an actor who would come in and would run around the room several times before auditioning. I think it was his way of getting rid of tension. It didn't really bother me, and, although it was kooky, I appreciated that he felt free enough to do that.

Representation

Nicole Astell – Prestige Management NYC

How and why did you become a manager?

I sort of fell into it. I went to school at the University of Iowa for theatre and cinema production and then when it came time to graduate I had no idea what I was going to do. My actor friends at college told me I would make a great agent, but I really liked casting and directing, so I came out to New York and did an internship with Liz Lewis Casting. I thought casting was really interesting, so I did another internship at Paladino Casting, and then I got hired at a modeling agency in Pennsylvania to start up their acting division. I came to the conclusion I didn't like being an agent because there were so many clients, but I really cared about my actors and didn't want to leave them. I moved back to New York and Prestige Management hired me to help with the children's division and let me build my adult roster in the process. Now I get the chance to work with only the clients I want and keep my roster to a reasonable number.

Briefly, what is the difference between a manger and an agent? What exactly does a manager do?

The most frequently asked question. Ultimately it comes down to this: an agent HAS TO LEGALLY find you work, while a manager's job is to get you prepared for auditions, manage your auditions/calendars, and find you agents. Managers and agents work hand-in-hand. Managers have smaller rosters than agents, so managers are able to really focus on their client, their brand, and managing the client's career.

Where do you find new clients?

Most of my clients I find at industry workshops or they are referred by my current clients.

Aside from exclusivity/a contract, what is the difference in your mind between freelancing with someone and signing them?

I like to say, "you don't get married on a first date". I think it's always best to freelance with people first because you want to make sure that you're a good match and could have a successful future together. But honestly, in my mind, there isn't a difference between a freelance client and a signed client. I treat them the same and do the same work for both of them.

I have some talented friends with representation, but the people they freelance with seem to rarely send them out. What advice do you have for them? Should they just keep looking for new representation?

In my opinion, it's best to find management representation because their rosters are smaller than an agency rosters and sometimes clients can get over looked. It's never a bad thing to keep seeking representation because maybe your current match isn't the best one for you. Always take classes with casting directors so you get in front of them and they can get to know who you are as an actor because your representation may be submitting you a lot, but doesn't get auditions for you because the casting directors don't know who you are.

What are your thoughts on mailings, and what do you think is appropriate/useful for prospective clients to send?

I don't like mailings and I feel bad saying that because I know it's what actors are taught to do. Honestly, if you just send me your headshot and resume, it will probably end up in the trash because I need to see you PERFORM in order to judge whether or not you're a good fit for my roster. If you send me a showcase invite though, I'm more likely to go and scout there.

What do you think is the biggest misconception about managers actors have?

I think a lot of actors think you only need a manager "once you've made it big". That's wrong. It's best to have a manager in the beginning because they help you navigate this industry.

Any other advice to new actors, or to actors in general?

Do not join the union (SAG-AFTRA) until you have a solid on-camera resume. You need to have strong principal and supporting roles on your resume before you even consider it. Also - don't give up. This industry can be brutal and heartbreaking, but stick with it. Find the right people to help you and listen to their advice.

Jenevieve Brewer – Terrific Talent Associates

BIO

Jenevieve Brewer was a Legit, Commercial, & Print Agent with AboutFace where she handled clients for print as well as union and non-union for on-camera commercials & voice-overs. She has since started her own boutique management agency Terrific Talent Associates.

What was your path to becoming an agent?

I started as an intern working on soaps and then worked my way into the writing/production departments. I then went on to work at a larger agency before having the opportunity to start my own.

Why did you decide to represent clients for legit, commercials, AND print, and how do you manage to *do* all that?

I feel it's best for both the agency and the actors when you're a full service agency - that way your actors are able to reach their full booking potential. With a great, hardworking staff, it's manageable.

Why did you decide to become a manager?

I decided to go into boutique management so I could really focus on a select number of clients and push them to the next level and have more time to guide them and give them personal One-on-One attention. I also am doing more producing and I am currently producing the trailer for 'Alphabet City: A City Within A City' written by Nefertiti Jones.

Where do you find new clients?

Everywhere! Showcases, events, through the mail, recommendations from actors and casting directors, even on the street or at a local coffee shop! We're always looking for actors that excite us.

Approximately how many breakdowns come across your desk per day, and what percentage would you say are commercial vs. legit?

The amount of breakdowns varies day to day, but it's pretty equal ratio wise between legit and commercial.

Why is it seemingly harder to get clients in for legit auditions than for commercial?

Legit is more specific, and casting tends to see fewer actors than with commercial auditions.

Aside from exclusivity/a contract, what is the difference in your mind between freelancing with someone and signing with them? When do you think a freelancer is ready to be signed?

Working with an agency is like a marriage on a professional level. Freelancing is a great way to start out to ensure happiness on both ends of the relationship. Both the actor and the agent should feel satisfied with the partnership, and it takes time to explore that.

I have talented friends that freelance with agents/managers who seem to rarely send them out. What advice do you have for them? Should they just keep looking for new representation?

They have to be proactive on their end with networking to benefit both the agent and the client when it comes to submitting.

What are your thoughts on mailings, and what do you think is appropriate/useful for prospective clients to send?

We go through our mail daily and find many clients that way. A simple headshot and resume suffice!

Any other advice to actors just starting out, or to actors in general?

Being as proactive as you can with networking and being the best version of you possible. Also be persistent and don't give up. Sometimes it takes time to incorporate new talent into our roster due to the existing talent we currently represent, so being patient is key.

Phil Cassese – Stewart Talent

BIO

After graduating with a BA in music from SUNY Stony Brook, Phil began his entertainment career at Arabesque Records. Cassese spent four years overseeing the marketing, advertising, promotion and publicity duties for Arabesque. While there, Phil worked closely with well-known jazz and classical artists such as Dave Douglas, Art Farmer, Charles McPherson, and others.

After Arabesque records, Cassese was recruited to work with Joel Dorn's 32 Records (famous for it's "Jazz for A Rainy Afternoon" series). As publicity director, Phil released recordings by the late Woody Shaw, Tom Jones and Judy Garland. Additionally, Phil co-produced several recordings with Todd Barkan (currently creative director for Jazz At Lincoln Center).

While still holding a full-time position, Cassese completed his Master's in Media at the New School University and created his own management company called Genuine Artist Management.

Phil Cassese heads the on-camera commercial division of Stewart Talent's New York office. He previously held the same position at TalentWorks where he spent six years developing a highly competitive roster of talent. His interest in comedy led him to develop a strong roster of improvisers and comedic actors.

Phil also teaches acting for commercials at The Upright Citizen's Brigade, NYU's Stonestreet Program, and One-on-One Productions.

Where do you find new clients?

Everywhere. With commercials, there's no barrier to entry with your look. I've approached bands, acrobats, other specialty talent. Word of mouth, casting directors, and other clients are good places for recommendations. I've given my card to bands in the subway, told them to contact me for an audition, and they booked it. The more you're performing, the better chance you'll be seen. Agents tend to go to shows their clients are in that have more people in them so they can see more performers.

What trends (if any) have you noticed in breakdowns lately?

Improv definitely. It might be more than a trend though. Comedy is used to sell products all the time, but improvisers can bring the most real performance, add new things to a script, elevate the copy, make it their own, and make it better. All kinds of happy accidents happen when you're just riffing off the top of your head or improvising a scene, and directors and ad agencies love that. So many breakdowns each day say 'Great with comedic improv.'

Whatever is hot on tv or in the movies seems to end up becoming a trend in the breakdowns. So Zooey Deschanel is a big prototype right now as well as Paul Rudd, and Ty Burrell from *Modern Family*. Napoleon Dynamite was big for a while. *Sex in the City* girls were hot for a while as a prototype for breakdowns. Glasses for girls, even guys, a little nerdy, redheads... all seem to be in vogue these days.

Aside from exclusivity/a contract, what is the difference in your mind between freelancing with someone and signing them?

I used freelancers at Talentworks for six years, and I signed a core group of people. But I found my roster was so bloated with people that when I moved over to Stewart Talent, I had this massive list of clients, and I was sending this huge list of names to casting directors. I think it was overwhelming for them, and it was overwhelming for me. Breakdowns just took too long to do. I had too many people and not a lot of them were getting time. So I stopped freelancing and I became 'signed only' which a few of the agencies in the city are, and I think all agents in LA are 'signed only'. But I think as a new actor learning the commercial game, you need a consistent amount of auditions over a long period of time to get the hang of it, to get the ropes down, to get the casting directors to realize that you're good, and they want you in their castings all the time because you're going to make them look good to their directors and their ad agencies that they work with over and over again. That takes time. You have to learn how to take the right risks in those rooms and not be too safe. If you have an agent who's signed you for the longhaul and supported you through the ups and downs and the slow periods, then you can after a while get everything straight and right and get everybody on your side where you're starting to generate your own appointments.

In the beginning I can send someone into these rooms and push them and get them appointments, but after a while they've done enough things right in those rooms where they're being invited back and picked off my list more easily because now the casting director is a fan of theirs, and they've gotten certain directors on their side. If you can repeat that process through several casting offices, the busy ones in the city, then you're going to be called in all the time. Then you've got a lot of auditions and you can cut down that element of randomness that exists in commercials because it's so tough to be the one person that books the job. But with freelancing I feel that you don't necessarily get that many opportunities. You're meeting so many people and it's easy to say to someone that you like and want to send on an audition or two, 'Hey, let me freelance with you, give it a whirl' and you send them out a couple of times, but then you have all these other people you've taken on as freelancers, and it goes in a rotation and you get lost in the shuffle more easily.

An actor's goal should definitely be to get signed somewhere. Every agent freelances with specialty people, but they're not going to send out a lot of fire-breathers. But for the most part I think signing gives the actor a better chance to have more auditions over the long haul.

Now that you're with Stewart and you no longer freelance, how do you make the decision to sign someone you meet or see in a show?

You don't always get it right, but I feel like you have to make decisions and trust your judgement, and make a leap of faith. And if you've done it long enough, hopefully you get it right more times than others. I just go on an instinct. If you see someone act or perform, you can tell if they're good. It doesn't mean they're always going to become great commercial successes, but bottom line, sending someone who is a good actor, even if they don't figure it out commercially, at least the casting director won't hold it against you because they can appreciate that the person is talented. And some people are super, funny talented, and they just need that time to figure it out, and everyone's willing to give them that time because they *are* talented. Basically, a huge part of it is talent and ability and the right look, but then I just want to like somebody from a personal standpoint. I don't want to work with someone that I don't genuinely like or that I'm not charmed by or think is funny, or, whatever, because if I think about them in a positive light, and I send them to the casting directors, then hopefully the casting directors are going to see something of what I saw as well. And at the very bottom line, if they're not getting it done and not getting callbacks and everything, then at least they're likable, and you can protect yourself a little bit as far as that goes. It just makes your day way easier when you can call someone with an appointment or deal with someone on detailed things and like the interactions that you have with them. As opposed to not wanting to pick up the phone cause I know this person is going to talk my ear off, or he's just not a nice person, or mean, or bitter. All those things; you just try to avoid. There are so many talented people, if you can work with people that you really like then you make your life a lot easier and fun.

I have talented friends that would like to do commercials, but the people they freelance with seem to rarely send them out. What advice do you have for them? Should they just keep looking for new representation?

It all goes back to being seen as much as you can. So if you're performing at the PIT, you've got to invite as many people (audience and industry) to shows as you can. Keep improving, keep getting good at doing your shows, your improv, or whatever it is. Or branch out and do something theatrically. Do a straight (non-improv) show, too, or as many online videos and things that can go viral and get spread around. I, as an agent, am being sent clips all the time from my clients, and there are other people in those clips. I'm sending those clips to casting directors all the time to try to get them to see my clients, and they're going to see the *other* people in the clips. That goes for live shows, too. If I'm asked to go see something, I'm going to be looking at everyone in that show basically as a potential client.

Just because you happen to be freelancing with an agent, you can still do everything you can to try and get that agent to believe in you as much as you can to the point that they want to sign you. Let them know you're doing good work outside of their sending you out on auditions all of the time. The busier you are, the more the agent will appreciate that you're trying to make your own breaks. Send that stuff to other agents.

See if you have friends that have agents; ask the friend. What are you waiting for? You can't be too shy. You need people's help, that's why you have friends and that's why you're doing this. There's a right way to ask for help. If you know your friend has an agent say, 'Listen, I have this link to this video. Is there any chance you can send it to your agent for me?' or 'Can you get your agent down to this show we're doing on Thursday; are they coming at any time so I can prepare for that, and maybe shake their hand afterwards or buy them a drink?' You've got to ask for help. Probably some of the best clients I meet are from word-of-mouth from other clients that I love and respect. That happens a lot. They want to be helpful to their friends. Like you said, you know you have talented friends. Have them email me. It happens a lot like that.

What are your thoughts on mailings, and what do you think is appropriate/useful for prospective clients to send?

Mailings I feel are the nuts and bolts, daily work that you have to do as an actor. If you're calling yourself an actor that means you're up at 9am mailing postcards or going down to Equity open calls or auditioning for whatever you can. You're online looking through Actors Access or Casting Networks or Backstage.com, all three of which you should be a member of. I know actors who take the first hour and a half of each morning to look through all of those breakdowns and just self-submit and get auditions that way. That's great exercise as an actor.

The percentage of payback is pretty small probably, but, I, and other agents I know, definitely look through all their mail and call people in from that. So if you get one hit on forty postcards that you send, that's one more than you would have gotten.

I don't think a lot of agents appreciate being emailed, especially when you track down their email, and just send random emails cause their email boxes get very full. But if you go through the proper channels, and it's appropriate to do that in a very short concise way, and send the right kind of materials, then something good is bound to happen at some point.

If you're just always thinking about 'How can I get to these people...?' Actors Connection, One-on-One, are places where you can get right in front of these agents and casting directors. If you're good, they're going to want to work with you and call you in. It's going to happen. So some of those things can be really worth it. A Brooke and Mary Class, Stacy Gallo's class at One-on-One, take the right classes with the right casting directors. Only take those classes with people that are working in the industry now. Those are the people that can help you, who know what's going on, what the trends are right now. All of that stuff combined.

I have clients that make sure if they bartend, they bartend at a restaurant or bar in the theater district where the Broadway people are coming in, where the actors and casts of these shows are coming in. They're just around it all the time. Those little things, they're intangibles and they're leaps of faith, but you do them cause they're the right thing to do, and eventually they end up paying off if you're also good at what you do. If you suck, you can do that until you're 80 and you're not going to get much work out of it.

Any other advice to new actors, or to actors in general?

Be as friendly and open and out there as much as you can. Don't burn any bridges. Be nice to everybody. This is a super small industry. If you're on the phone with some person who's answering the phone at the casting director's office, be nice to them because they are the casting director of tomorrow. Assistants come up together, same as actors.

And perform as much as you can.

DAVID NEAL LEVIN

ABOUT THE AUTHOR

David Neal Levin is an actor and writer living in Brooklyn, NY. Originally from Nashville, he moved to New York after grad school and studied at Michael Howard Studios. His credits include '**Boardwalk Empire**', '**The Knick**', '**The Leftovers**', '**Onion News Network**', '**Adult Swim**', '**Orange is the New Black**', numerous commercials, and the movie '**The Golden Scallop**'.

David studied and still occasionally performs improv at the Magnet Theater in NYC.

You can learn more and see some of his work at www.davidneallevin.com.

CPSIA information can be obtained at www.ICGtesting.com
Printed in the USA
LVOW08s2014290316

481260LV00002BA/459/P

9 781505 345377